Ninja Foodi Grill Cookbook for Beginners

600 Air Frying and Indoor Grilling Recipes, with A 30 Days Diet plan

Louella Lucier

© **Copyright 2020 - All rights reserved.**

The content contained within this book may not be reproduced, duplicated or transmitted without direct written permission from the author or the publisher.

Under no circumstances will any blame or legal responsibility be held against the publisher, or author, for any damages, reparation, or monetary loss due to the information contained within this book, either directly or indirectly.

Legal Notice:

This book is copyright protected. It is only for personal use. You cannot amend, distribute, sell, use, quote or paraphrase any part, or the content within this book, without the consent of the author or publisher.

Disclaimer Notice:

Please note the information contained within this document is for educational and entertainment purposes only. All effort has been executed to present accurate, up to date, reliable, complete information. No warranties of any kind are declared or implied. Readers acknowledge that the author is not engaged in the rendering of legal, financial, medical or professional advice. The content within this book has been derived from various sources. Please consult a licensed professional before attempting any techniques outlined in this book.

By reading this document, the reader agrees that under no circumstances is the author responsible for any losses, direct or indirect, that are incurred as a result of the use of the information contained within this document, including, but not limited to, errors, omissions, or inaccuracies.

Table of Contents

Introduction..4
   The Ninja Foodi Grill Features & Functions.....................4
   Working of the Ninja Foodi Grill...........5

Breakfast Recipes.....................................7
   Spinach & Turkey Bites...........................8
   Mushroom Frittata.....................................9
   Sausage & Scallion Frittata...................10
   Chicken & Broccoli Quiche...................11
   Eggs with Ham..12
   Savory Carrot Muffins...........................13
   Pumpkin Bread...15
   Bacon & Kale Cups..................................16

Snacks & Appetizer Recipes..................17
   Pumpkin Fries..18
   Apple Chips..19
   Cheddar Meatballs................................20
   BBQ Chicken Wings..............................21
   Chicken Nuggets....................................22
   Little Smokies..23
   Crispy Shrimp..24
   Bacon-Wrapped Shrimp......................25
   Mozzarella Flatbread............................26
   Onion Dip...27
   Spinach Dip..28

Sides & Vegetable Recipes...................29
   Stuffed Tomatoes...................................59
   Herbed Mushrooms..............................60
   Glazed Carrots..61
   Lemony Green Beans..........................62
   Vinegar Brussels Sprout.......................63
   Nutty Acorn Squash..............................64
   Stuffed Potatoes.....................................65
   Vegetarian Stuffed Bell Peppers.........67
   Green Beans Casserole.......................68
   Tofu with Orange Sauce......................69

Fish & Seafood Recipes........................29
   Zesty Salmon..30
   Glazed Salmon.......................................31
   Teriyaki Salmon......................................32
   Glazed Haddock....................................33
   Buttered Halibut.....................................34
   Spiced Tilapia...35
   Parmesan Shrimp.................................36
   Shrimp Kabobs......................................37
   Shrimp Scampi......................................38
   Rosemary Scallops...............................39

   Scallops in Capers Sauce...................40
   Glazed Calamari....................................41

Poultry Mains Recipes..........................42
   Roasted Cornish Hen............................43
   Roasted Chicken with Potatoes.........44
   Spicy Roasted Chicken........................45
   Sweet & Spicy Chicken Drumsticks......46
   BBQ Chicken Breasts..........................47
   Sausage Stuffed Chicken Breast........48
   Spinach Stuffed Chicken Breasts......49
   Buttermilk Brined Turkey Breast.........50
   Buttered Turkey Breast........................51
   Thyme Turkey Tenderloins..................52
   Turkey Roll...53
   Turkey & Yogurt Casserole................55
   Turkey Meatloaf.....................................56
   Glazed Duck Breasts...........................57

Beef, Pork & Lamb Recipes.................70
   Herbed Beef Roast...............................71
   Bacon-Wrapped Beef Tenderloin......72
   Seasoned Rib-Eye Steak....................73
   Beef Casserole......................................74
   Beef Stuffed Bell Peppers...................75
   Glazed Pork Ribs..................................76
   Pork Loin with Potatoes......................77
   Garlicky Pork Tenderloin.....................78
   Glazed Ham..79
   Pork & Sausage Meatloaf...................80
   Glazed Leg of Lamb.............................81
   Pesto Rack of Lamb.............................82
   Garlicky Lamb Chops...........................83
   Sweet & Sour Lamb Chops................84

Dessert Recipes......................................85
   Stuffed Apples...86
   Cranberry Cupcakes............................87
   Chocolate Muffins..................................88
   Lava Cake...89
   Chocolate Brownie Cake.....................90
   Pumpkin Cake..91
   Mini Cheesecakes................................93
   Pumpkin Pie..94
   Pecan Pie...95
   Apple Bread Pudding...........................96
   Pumpkin Bread Pudding.....................98

Meal Plan for 30 Days..........................100

Conclusion..105

Introduction

Becoming "Smart" has changed the entire narrative and overall lifestyle of man in the modern-day world. From gadgets to appliances, to "Smart" automated homes, the 21st-century lifestyle has got stern domination of the internet. Considering the reach of the technological advancements, our kitchen has also been impacted very much overtime with the introduction of Smart devices & appliances for cooking. The Ninja Foodi Grill is one such Smart device that has changed the horizons of the cooking world. This is because it can perform grilling, baking, roasting, dehydrating, and air crisping, etc. The amalgamation of so many cooking techniques in one single device is a significant breakthrough in the cooking world. This is why the Ninja Foodi Grill is going to knock out all other conventional cooking appliances from your kitchen. Furthermore, it is certified as "smoke-free," giving you an ultra-convenient and healthy cooking solution.

The Ninja Foodi Grill preserves the originality of your ingredients by not altering its aroma or natural taste at all. The overall natural flavor of the ingredients is well maintained while cooking with the Ninja Foodi Grill. The perfect and suitable cooking temperature range is very beneficial in giving your food the perfect crispiness and tenderness. Without a doubt, the Ninja Foodi Grill has been very vital in redefining cooking experiences for its users. You can easily refer to it as the single ultimate and the perfect choice for almost all your cooking techniques and modes. It is built with various modern and crucial functions and features, which leads it ahead of its competitors and other cooking appliances.

The Ninja Foodi Grill Features & Functions

The salient features of the Ninja Foodi Grill are given as follows:

- he roasting capacity of up to 3 pounds.
- Smoke-free.
- Dishwasher safe certification.
- Easily cleanable.
- Can be utilized as a 4 Quarts Air Fryer.
- Searing is done by air circulation of 500° Fahrenheit hot air.
- Defrost your food in approximately 25 minutes.
- Performs air frying with a stunning 75 percent lesser fat than the traditional deep-frying technique.
- The size of the unit is 10 inches x 10 inches.
- The inner pot is non-stick and ceramic coated.

The salient functions of the Ninja Foodi Grill are given as follows:

1. Roast

2. Grill
3. Bake
4. Air crisp
5. Dehydrate

Working of the Ninja Foodi Grill

Grilling

The grilling function performs well both on frozen and regular meats. Chicken breasts, hamburgers, and steaks are grilled thoroughly with effective grilling. The grilling is even, well browned, crispy, and appears to be similar to regular grilling. Moreover, you don't need to flip the meats inside to achieve even and thorough grilling.

Preheating is required for the grilling function. Usually, the preheating time is approximately 8 minutes. The grilling function is considered the best for steaks as it beats steaks broiled in regular ovens. Moreover, the entire grilling process is some-free.

Air Frying

The Air frying option of the Ninja Foodi Grill makes the perfect fries both fresh and frozen. They are similar to the fast-food joint's fries everyone goes crazy about. It is significantly easier than regular air fryers to flip ingredients in the basket. The Ninja Food Grill's lid is opened in an upward direction, which makes it very easy to flip or move inside the crisper basket while air frying.

Roasting

You can easily roast a small piece of meat on your Ninja Foodi Grill. The final results have juiciness and tenderness, with a touch of a crackling crust.

Baking

The inner pot can easily fit an 8-inch pan, which can be used even to bake a cake in the Ninja Foodi Grill. The final product might have brownness and a moist, tender crumb too.

Dehydrating

The Ninja Foodi Grill is very useful in performing dehydration of food items. An apple will take around 7 hours to get thoroughly dehydrated with the Ninja Foodi Grill. But, considering the size, around 18 slices of apple can be fitted inside the Ninja Foodi Grill, which will yield approximately 1 ½ cup of dried apple rings.

Tips & Tricks for Cooking

Although the Ninja Foodi Grill is not hard to use at all. Yet, with a few tricks and tips, you can eventually become a pro at using the device best suited to your needs. These tricks and tips are focused on the various cooking modes of the Ninja Foodi Grill and will eventually yield you the perfect results. Keenly following these tips and tricks will give you the best possible results with the Ninja Foodi Grill. They are stated as follows:

Air Crisp

- If you coat your veggies and other ingredients thoroughly with oil before proceeding to air crisp them. This will provide them with the most perfect crispiness possible. The final product will be having significant crispiness with perfection.
- Perfect browning can be efficiently achieved by placing all your veggies and the rest of the ingredients evenly inside the Cook & Crisp Basket. This even placement is very vital in providing your ingredients the perfect browning possible.

Bake & Roast

- When you are using the Ninja Foodi Grill, always use the Ninja Multi-purpose Pan. The regular baking will not yield as good results as with the Ninja Multi-purpose Pan.

Dehydrate

- Always thoroughly dry your food before putting it inside the Cook & Crisp Basket.
- It is very vital to remember that almost every vegetable and fruit will take around 6 to 8 hours for dehydration. Moreover, jerky is going to take 5 to 7 hours for thorough dehydration. For a better idea, dehydration is directly proportional to the overall crispiness of your food. The more you dehydrate your food, the crispier it is going to be.
- You can thoroughly pasteurize all the ingredients by using the Roast function for approximately 1 minute at a temperature range of 300° Fahrenheit. This will be very vital and useful when your recipe involves dehydrated fish or meats. This trick is going to yield you the best results.
- You can place the veggies and fruits in a flat and closer order for generating more space inside the main pot. But you cannot or should not overlap them or even proceed to stack them as it is going to give you unevenly cooked ingredients.

Breakfast Recipes

Spinach & Turkey Bites

Preparation Time: 10 minutes
Cooking Time: 23 minutes
Servings: 4

Ingredients:

- 1 tablespoon unsalted butter
- 1 pound fresh baby spinach
- 4 eggs
- 7 ounces cooked turkey, chopped
- 4 teaspoons unsweetened almond milk
- Salt and freshly ground black pepper, to taste

Preparation:

1. In a frying pan, melt the butter over medium heat and cook the spinach for about 2-3 minutes or until just wilted.
2. Remove from the heat and drain the liquid completely.
3. Transfer the spinach into a bowl and set aside to cool slightly.
4. Arrange the "Crisper Basket" in the pot of Ninja Foodi Grill.
5. Close the Ninja Foodi Grill with lid and select "Air Crisp".
6. Set the temperature to 355 degrees F to preheat.
7. Press "Start/Stop" to begin preheating.
8. Divide the spinach into 4 greased ramekins, followed by the turkey.
9. Crack 1 egg into each ramekin and drizzle with almond milk.
10. Sprinkle with salt and black pepper.
11. When the display shows "Add Food" open the lid and place the ramekins into the "Crisper Basket".
12. Close the Ninja Foodi Grill with lid and set the time for 20 minutes.
13. Press "Start/Stop" to begin cooking.
14. When cooking time is completed, press "Start/Stop" to stop cooking and open the lid.
15. Serve hot.

Serving Suggestions: Serve alongside the fresh greens.

Variation Tip: Spinach can be replaced with any leafy green.

Nutritional Information per Serving:

Calories: 200 | **Fat:** 10.2g | **Sat Fat:** 4.1g | **Carbohydrates:** 4.5g | **Fiber:** 2.5g | **Sugar:** 0.8g | **Protein:** 23.4g

Mushroom Frittata

Preparation Time: 15 minutes
Cooking Time: 14 minutes
Servings: 2

Ingredients:

- 1 bacon slice, chopped
- 6 cherry tomatoes, halved
- 6 fresh mushrooms, sliced
- Salt and freshly ground black pepper, to taste
- 3 eggs
- 1 tablespoon fresh parsley, chopped
- ½ cup Parmesan cheese, grated

Preparation:

1. In a baking pan, add the bacon, tomatoes, mushrooms, salt, and black pepper and mix well.
2. Arrange the "Crisper Basket" in the pot of Ninja Foodi Grill.
3. Close the Ninja Foodi Grill with lid and select "Air Crisp".
4. Set the temperature to 320 degrees F to preheat.
5. Press "Start/Stop" to begin preheating.
6. When the display shows "Add Food" open the lid and place the pan into the "Crisper Basket".
7. Close the Ninja Foodi Grill with lid and set the time for 14 minutes.
8. Press "Start/Stop" to begin cooking.
9. Meanwhile, in a bowl, add the eggs and beat well.
10. Add in the parsley and cheese and mix well.
11. After 6 minutes, top the bacon mixture with egg mixture evenly.
12. When the cooking time is completed, press "Start/Stop" to stop cooking and open the lid.
13. Serve hot.

Serving Suggestions: Enjoy your frittata with the drizzling of melted butter.

Variation Tip: Any flavored cheese will be terrific here.

Nutritional Information per Serving:

Calories: 489 | **Fat:** 35.8g|**Sat Fat:** 15.1g|**Carbohydrates:** 7.5g|**Fiber:** 0.9g|**Sugar:** 2.1g|**Protein:** 39.6g

Sausage & Scallion Frittata

Preparation Time: 10 minutes
Cooking Time: 20 minutes
Servings: 2

Ingredients:

- ¼ pound cooked turkey sausage, crumbled
- ½ cup Cheddar cheese, shredded
- 4 eggs, beaten lightly
- 2 scallions, chopped
- Pinch of cayenne pepper

Preparation:

1. In a bowl, add the sausage, cheese, eggs, scallion and cayenne and mix until well combined.
2. Place the mixture into a greased 6x2-inch cake pan.
3. Arrange the "Crisper Basket" in the pot of Ninja Foodi Grill.
4. Close the Ninja Foodi Grill with lid and select "Air Crisp".
5. Set the temperature to 360 degrees F to preheat.
6. Press "Start/Stop" to begin preheating.
7. When the display shows "Add Food" open the lid and place the pan into the "Crisper Basket".
8. Close the Ninja Foodi Grill with lid and set the time for 20 minutes.
9. Press "Start/Stop" to begin cooking.
10. When cooking time is completed, press "Start/Stop" to stop cooking and open the lid.
11. Serve hot.

Serving Suggestions: Avocado slices will go great with frittata

Variation Tip: Pick the right cheese for the frittata.

Nutritional Information per Serving:

Calories: 437 | **Fat:** 34.2g | **Sat Fat:** 13.9g | **Carbohydrates:** 2.2g | **Fiber:** 0.4g | **Sugar:** 1.2g | **Protein:** 29.4g

Chicken & Broccoli Quiche

Preparation Time: 15 minutes
Cooking Time: 12 minutes
Servings: 2

Ingredients:

- ½ of frozen ready-made pie crust
- ¼ tablespoon olive oil
- 1 small egg
- 3 tablespoons cheddar cheese, grated
- 1½ tablespoons whipping cream
- Salt and freshly ground black pepper, to taste
- 3 tablespoons boiled broccoli, chopped
- 2 tablespoons cooked chicken, chopped

Preparation:

1. Cut 1 (5-inch) round from the pie crust.
2. Arrange the pie crust round in a small pie pan and gently press in the bottom and sides.
3. In a bowl, mix together the egg, cheese, cream, salt, and black pepper.
4. Pour the egg mixture over dough base and top with the broccoli and chicken.
5. Arrange the "Crisper Basket" in the pot of Ninja Foodi Grill.
6. Close the Ninja Foodi Grill with lid and select "Air Crisp".
7. Set the temperature to 390 degrees F to preheat.
8. Press "Start/Stop" to begin preheating.
9. When the display shows "Add Food" open the lid and place the pan into the "Crisper Basket".
10. Close the Ninja Foodi Grill with lid and set the time for 12 minutes.
11. Press "Start/Stop" to begin cooking.
12. When cooking time is completed, press "Start/Stop" to stop cooking and open the lid.
13. Cut into equal-sized wedges and serve.

Serving Suggestions: Serve with the garnishing of fresh herbs.

Variation Tip: Make sure your fillings are as dry as possible.

Nutritional Information per Serving:

Calories: 197 | **Fat:** 15g | **Sat Fat:** 5.9g | **Carbohydrates:** 9g | **Fiber:** 0.4g | **Sugar:** 0.9g | **Protein:** 8.6g

Eggs with Ham

Preparation Time: 10 minutes
Cooking Time: 13 minutes
Servings: 2

Ingredients:

- 2 teaspoons unsalted butter, softened
- 2 ounces ham, sliced thinly
- 4 large eggs, divided
- Salt and freshly ground black pepper, to taste
- 2 tablespoons heavy cream
- 1/8 teaspoon smoked paprika
- 3 tablespoons Parmesan cheese, grated finely
- 2 teaspoons fresh chives, minced

Preparation:

1. Arrange the "Crisper Basket" in the pot of Ninja Foodi Grill.
2. Close the Ninja Foodi Grill with lid and select "Air Crisp".
3. Set the temperature to 320 degrees F to preheat.
4. Press "Start/Stop" to begin preheating.
5. In the bottom of a baking pan, spread butter.
6. Arrange the ham slices over the butter.
7. In a bowl, add 1 egg, salt, black pepper and cream and beat until smooth.
8. Place the egg mixture over the ham slices evenly.
9. Carefully crack the remaining eggs on top and sprinkle with paprika, salt, black pepper, cheese and chives evenly.
10. When the display shows "Add Food" open the lid and place the pan into the "Crisper Basket".
11. Close the Ninja Foodi Grill with lid and set the time for 13 minutes.
12. Press "Start/Stop" to begin cooking.
13. When cooking time is completed, press "Start/Stop" to stop cooking and open the lid.
14. Cut into equal-sized wedges and serve.

Serving Suggestions: Toasted bread slices will go great.

Variation Tip: Use freshly shredded cheese.

Nutritional Information per Serving:

Calories: 302 | **Fat:** 23.6g | **Sat Fat:** 10.7g | **Carbohydrates:** 2.4g | **Fiber:** 0.5g | **Sugar:** 0.8g | **Protein:** 20.7g

Savory Carrot Muffins

Preparation Time: 15 minutes
Cooking Time: 7 minutes
Servings: 6

Ingredients:

- 1¼ cup whole-wheat flour
- ¼ cup all-purpose flour
- ½ teaspoon baking powder
- 1/8 teaspoon baking soda
- ½ teaspoon dried parsley, crushed
- ¼ teaspoon salt
- ½ cup yogurt
- 1 teaspoon balsamic vinegar
- 1 tablespoon vegetable oil
- 3 tablespoons cottage cheese, grated
- 1 carrot, peeled and grated
- 2-4 tablespoons water (if needed)
- 7 ounces Parmesan cheese, grated
- ¼ cup walnuts, chopped

Preparation:

1. Grease 6 medium muffin molds.
2. In a large bowl, mix together the flours, baking powder, baking soda, parsley, and salt.
3. In another large bowl, add the yogurt and vinegar and mix well.
4. Add the oil, cottage cheese and carrot and mix well. (Add some water if needed).
5. Make a well in the center of the yogurt mixture.
6. Slowly, add the flour mixture in the well and mix until well combined.
7. Place the mixture into the prepared muffin molds evenly and top with the Parmesan cheese and walnuts.
8. Arrange the "Crisper Basket" in the pot of Ninja Foodi Grill.
9. Close the Ninja Foodi Grill with lid and select "Air Crisp".
10. Set the temperature to 355 degrees F to preheat.
11. Press "Start/Stop" to begin preheating.
12. When the display shows "Add Food" open the lid and place the muffin molds into the "Crisper Basket".
13. Close the Ninja Foodi Grill with lid and set the time for 7 minutes.
14. Press "Start/Stop" to begin cooking.

15. When the cooking time is completed, press "Start/Stop" to stop cooking and open the lid.
16. Place the muffin molds onto a wire rack for about 10 minutes.
17. Carefully, invert the muffins onto the wire rack to cool completely before serving.

Serving Suggestions: Serve with the drizzling of melted butter.

Variation Tip: You can add some sweetener according to your taste.

Nutritional Information per Serving:

Calories: 222 | **Fat:** 12.9g|**Sat Fat:** 5.7g|**Carbohydrates:** 12.6g|**Fiber:** 0.9g| **Sugar:** 2g|**Protein:** 15.2g

Pumpkin Bread

Preparation Time: 10 minutes
Cooking Time: 25 minutes
Servings: 4

Ingredients:

- ¼ cup coconut flour
- 2 tablespoons stevia blend
- 1 teaspoon baking powder
- ¾ teaspoon pumpkin pie spice
- ¼ teaspoon ground cinnamon
- 1/8 teaspoon salt
- ¼ cup canned pumpkin
- 2 large eggs

- 2 tablespoons unsweetened almond milk
- 1 teaspoon vanilla extract

Preparation:

1. In a bowl, add the flour, stevia blend, baking powder, spices and salt and mix well.
2. In another large bowl, add the pumpkin, eggs, almond milk, and vanilla extract. Beat until well combined.
3. Add the flour mixture and mix until just combined.
4. Arrange the "Crisper Basket" in the pot of Ninja Foodi Grill.
5. Close the Ninja Foodi Grill with lid and select "Air Crisp".
6. Set the temperature to 350 degrees F to preheat.
7. Press "Start/Stop" to begin preheating.
8. Place the mixture into a greased parchment paper lined cake pan evenly.
9. When the display shows "Add Food" open the lid and place the pan into the "Crisper Basket".
10. Close the Ninja Foodi Grill with lid and set the time for 25 minutes.
11. Press "Start/Stop" to begin cooking.
12. When cooking time is completed, press "Start/Stop" to stop cooking and open the lid.
13. Place the bread pan onto a wire rack for about 5-10 minutes.
14. Carefully remove the bread from pan and place onto a wire rack to cool completely before slicing.
15. Cut the bread into desired-sized slices and serve.

Serving Suggestions: Enjoy this bread with cranberry jam.

Variation Tip: Unsweetened almond milk can be replaced with coconut milk.

Nutritional Information per Serving:

Calories: 78 | **Fat:** 3.4g | **Sat Fat:** 1.3g | **Carbohydrates:** 7.5g | **Fiber:** 3.6g | **Sugar:** 0.9g | **Protein:** 4.4g

Bacon & Kale Cups

Preparation Time: 10 minutes
Cooking Time: 17 minutes
Servings: 6

Ingredients:

- 6 eggs
- ½ cup milk
- Salt and freshly ground black pepper, to taste
- 1 cup fresh kale, tough ribs removed and chopped
- 4 cooked bacon slices, crumbled

Preparation:

1. Arrange the "Crisper Basket" in the pot of Ninja Foodi Grill.
2. Close the Ninja Foodi Grill with lid and select "Air Crisp".
3. Set the temperature to 325 degrees F to preheat.
4. Press "Start/Stop" to begin preheating.
5. In a bowl, add the eggs, milk, salt and black pepper and beat until well combined.
6. Add the kale and stir to combine.
7. Divide the kale mixture into 6 greased cups.
8. When the display shows "Add Food" open the lid and place the cups into the "Crisper Basket".
9. Close the Ninja Foodi Grill with lid and set the time for 17 minutes.
10. Press "Start/Stop" to begin cooking.
11. When the cooking time is completed, press "Start/Stop" to stop cooking and open the lid.
12. Serve with the topping of bacon pieces.

Serving Suggestions: Serve with the garnishing of Parmesan cheese.

Variation Tip: Don't overcook the cups.

Nutritional Information per Serving:

Calories: 183 | **Fat:** 12.9g|**Sat Fat:** 4.3g|**Carbohydrates:** 2.8g|**Fiber:** 0.2g|**Sugar:** 1.3g|**Protein:** 13.7g

Snacks & Appetizer Recipes

Pumpkin Fries

Preparation Time: 10 minutes
Cooking Time: 35 minutes
Servings: 2

Ingredients:

- 14 ounces pumpkin, peeled and cut into strips
- 2 teaspoons olive oil
- ½ teaspoon ground cinnamon
- ½ teaspoon red chili powder
- ¼ teaspoon garlic salt
- Salt and freshly ground black pepper, to taste

Preparation:

1. In a bowl, add all the ingredients and toss to coat well.
2. Arrange the greased "Crisper Basket" in the pot of Ninja Foodi Grill.
3. Close the Ninja Foodi Grill with lid and select "Air Crisp".
4. Set the temperature to 400 degrees F to preheat.
5. Press "Start/Stop" to begin preheating.
6. When the display shows "Add Food" open the lid and arrange the fries in "Crisper Basket".
7. Close the Ninja Foodi Grill with lid and set the time for 30 minutes.
8. Press "Start/Stop" to begin cooking.
9. When cooking time is completed, press "Start/Stop" to stop cooking and open the lid.
10. Serve warm.

Serving Suggestions: Enjoy these fries with ketchup.

Variation Tip: Adjust the ratio of spices according to your taste.

Nutritional Information per Serving:

Calories: 112 | **Fat:** 5.4g|**Sat Fat:** 1g|**Carbohydrates:** 17.1g|**Fiber:** 6.3g|**Sugar:** 6.7g|**Protein:** 2.3g

Apple Chips

Preparation Time: 10 minutes
Cooking Time: 8 minutes
Servings: 2

Ingredients:

- 1 apple, peeled, cored and thinly sliced
- 1 tablespoon sugar
- ½ teaspoon ground cinnamon
- Pinch of ground cardamom
- Pinch of ground ginger
- Pinch of salt

Preparation:

1. In a bowl, add all the ingredients and toss to coat well.
2. Arrange the greased "Crisper Basket" in the pot of Ninja Foodi Grill.
3. Close the Ninja Foodi Grill with lid and select "Air Crisp".
4. Set the temperature to 390 degrees F to preheat.
5. Press "Start/Stop" to begin preheating.
6. When the display shows "Add Food" open the lid and arrange the apple chips in "Crisper Basket".
7. Close the Ninja Foodi Grill with lid and set the time for 6 minutes.
8. Press "Start/Stop" to begin cooking.
9. When cooking time is completed, press "Start/Stop" to stop cooking and open the lid.
10. Set the apple chips aside to cool before serving.

Serving Suggestions: Serve with the sprinkling of extra cinnamon.

Variation Tip: Make sure to pat dry the apple slices before cooking.

Nutritional Information per Serving:

Calories: 83 | **Fat:** 0.2g|**Sat Fat:** 0g|**Carbohydrates:** 22g|**Fiber:** 3.1g|**Sugar:** 17.6g|**Protein:** 0.3g

Cheddar Meatballs

Preparation Time: 15 minutes
Cooking Time: 14 minutes
Servings: 2

Ingredients:

- ½ pound ground turkey
- 1 onion, chopped
- 1 teaspoon garlic paste
- 2 tablespoons fresh basil, chopped
- 1 teaspoon mustard
- 1 teaspoon maple syrup
- 1 tablespoon Cheddar cheese, grated
- Salt and freshly ground black pepper, to taste

Preparation:

1. In a bowl, add all ingredients and mix until well combined.
2. Make small equal-sized balls from the mixture.
3. Arrange the greased "Crisper Basket" in the pot of Ninja Foodi Grill.
4. Close the Ninja Foodi Grill with lid and select "Air Crisp".
5. Set the temperature to 390 degrees F to preheat.
6. Press "Start/Stop" to begin preheating.
7. When the display shows "Add Food" open the lid and arrange the meatballs in "Crisper Basket".
8. Close the Ninja Foodi Grill with lid and set the time for 14 minutes.
9. Press "Start/Stop" to begin cooking.
10. When cooking time is completed, press "Start/Stop" to stop cooking and open the lid.
11. Serve hot.

Serving Suggestions: Serve with your favorite dipping sauce.

Variation Tip: Fresh basil can be replaced with dried basil.

Nutritional Information per Serving:

Calories: 277 | **Fat:** 14.2g|**Sat Fat:** 2.8g|**Carbohydrates:** 8.5g|**Fiber:** 1.5g|**Sugar:** 4.5g|**Protein:** 33.1g

BBQ Chicken Wings

Preparation Time: 15 minutes
Cooking Time: 19 minutes
Servings: 4

Ingredients:

- 2 pounds chicken wings
- 1 teaspoon olive oil
- 1 teaspoon smoked paprika
- 1 teaspoon garlic powder
- Salt and freshly ground black pepper, to taste
- ¼ cup barbecue sauce

Preparation:

1. Arrange the "Crisper Basket" in the pot of Ninja Foodi Grill.
2. Close the Ninja Foodi Grill with lid and select "Air Crisp".
3. Set the temperature to 360 degrees F to preheat.
4. Press "Start/Stop" to begin preheating.
5. In a large bowl combine chicken wings, smoked paprika, garlic powder, oil, salt, and black pepper and mix well.
6. When the display shows "Add Food" open the lid and place the chicken wings the "Crisper Basket" in a single layer.
7. Close the Ninja Foodi Grill with lid and select "Air Crisp".
8. Set the temperature to 360 degrees F for 19 minutes.
9. Press "Start/Stop" to begin cooking.
10. After 12 minutes of cooking, flip the wings and coat with barbecue sauce evenly.
11. When cooking time is completed, press "Start/Stop" to stop cooking and open the lid.
12. Serve immediately.

Serving Suggestions: Blue cheese dip will go great with these wings.

Variation Tip: You can use any kind of barbecue sauce.

Nutritional Information per Serving:

Calories: 468 | **Fat:** 18.1g | **Sat Fat:** 4.8g | **Carbohydrates:** 6.5g | **Fiber:** 0.4g | **Sugar:** 4.3g | **Protein:** 65.8g

Chicken Nuggets

Preparation Time: 20 minutes
Cooking Time: 10 minutes
Servings: 5

Ingredients:

- ½ of zucchini, chopped roughly
- ½ of carrot, peeled and chopped roughly
- 14 ounces boneless, skinless chicken breasts, cut into chunks
- ½ tablespoon mustard powder
- 1 tablespoon garlic powder
- 1 tablespoon onion powder
- Salt and ground black pepper, as required
- 1 cup all-purpose flour
- 2 tablespoons milk
- 1 egg
- 1 cup panko breadcrumbs

Preparation:

1. In a food processor, add zucchini and carrot and pulse until chopped finely.
2. Add the chicken, mustard powder, garlic powder, onion powder, salt and black pepper and pulse until just combined.
3. Make equal-sized nuggets from the mixture.
4. In a shallow dish, place the flour.
5. In a second shallow dish, beat the milk and egg.
6. In a third shallow dish, place the breadcrumbs.
7. Coat the nuggets with flour, then dip into egg mixture and finally, coat with the breadcrumbs.
8. Arrange the "Crisper Basket" in the pot of Ninja Foodi Ninja Foodi Grill with lid and select "Air Crisp".
9. Set the temperature to 390 degrees F to preheat.
10. Press "Start/Stop" to begin preheating.
11. When the display shows "Add Food" open the lid and place the nuggets into the "Crisper Basket" in a single layer.
12. Close the Ninja Foodi Grill with lid and set the time for 10 minutes.
13. Press "Start/Stop" to begin cooking.
14. When the cooking time is completed, press "Start/Stop" to stop cooking and open the lid.
15. Serve warm.

Serving Suggestions: Enjoy with mustard sauce.

Variation Tip: Crushed pork rinds can be used instead of breadcrumbs.

Nutritional Information per Serving:

Calories: 537 | **Fat:** 9g | **Sat Fat:** 2.6g | **Carbohydrates:** 26.7g | **Fiber:** 1.5g | **Sugar:** 2.1g | **Protein:** 28.4g

Little Smokies

Preparation Time: 15 minutes
Cooking Time: 10 minutes
Servings: 8

Ingredients:

- 2/3 pound bacon strips
- 14 ounces little smokies
- 1/3 cup brown sugar

Preparation:

1. Cut the bacon strips into thirds across the width.
2. In a shallow dish, place the brown sugar.
3. Coat both sides of bacon strips with brown sugar.
4. Wrap each smokie with a bacon piece.
5. Then secure each wrapped smokie with a toothpick.
6. Arrange the "Crisper Basket" in the pot of Ninja Foodi Grill.
7. Close the Ninja Foodi Grill with lid and select "Air Crisp".
8. Set the temperature to 350 degrees F to preheat.
9. Press "Start/Stop" to begin preheating.
10. When the display shows "Add Food" open the lid and arrange the wrapped smokies in "Crisper Basket" in a single layer.
11. Close the Ninja Foodi Grill with lid and set the time for 10 minutes.
12. Press "Start/Stop" to begin cooking.
13. Flip the smokies once halfway through.
14. When cooking time is completed, press "Start/Stop" to stop cooking and open the lid.

Serving Suggestions: Serve with the drizzling of fresh orange juice.

Variation Tip: You can cut back the ratio of sweetness.

Nutritional Information per Serving:

Calories: 384 | **Fat:** 30.6g|**Sat Fat:** 10.4g|**Carbohydrates:** 7.3g|**Fiber:** 0g|**Sugar:** 6.7g|**Protein:** 19.2g

Crispy Shrimp

Preparation Time: 20 minutes
Cooking Time: 20 minutes
Servings: 4

Ingredients:

- 1 pound shrimp, peeled and deveined
- Salt and freshly ground black pepper, to taste
- 8 ounces coconut milk
- ½ cup panko breadcrumbs
- ½ teaspoon cayenne pepper

Preparation:

1. In a shallow dish, mix together the coconut milk, salt and black pepper.
2. In another shallow dish, mix together breadcrumbs, cayenne pepper, salt and black pepper.
3. Dip the shrimp in coconut milk mixture and then coat with the breadcrumbs mixture.
4. Arrange the "Crisper Basket" in the pot of Ninja Foodi Grill.
5. Close the Ninja Foodi Grill with lid and select "Air Crisp".
6. Set the temperature to 350 degrees F to preheat.
7. Press "Start/Stop" to begin preheating.
8. When the display shows "Add Food" open the lid and place the shrimp into the "Crisper Basket".
9. Close the Ninja Foodi Grill with lid and set the time for 20 minutes.
10. Press "Start/Stop" to begin cooking.
11. When cooking time is completed, press "Start/Stop" to stop cooking and open the lid.
12. Serve warm.

Serving Suggestions: Serve with the drizzling of garlic butter.

Variation Tip: You may use regular breadcrumbs instead of panko.

Nutritional Information per Serving:

Calories: 301 | **Fat:** 15.7g | **Sat Fat:** 12.6g | **Carbohydrates:** 12.5g | **Fiber:** 2.3g | **Sugar:** 2.2g | **Protein:** 28.2g

Bacon-Wrapped Shrimp

Preparation Time: 15 minutes
Cooking Time: 7 minutes
Servings: 6

Ingredients:

- 1 pound bacon, thinly sliced
- 1 pound shrimp, peeled and deveined

Preparation:

1. Wrap each shrimp with one bacon slice.
2. Arrange the shrimp in a baking dish and refrigerate for about 20 minutes.
3. Arrange the "Crisper Basket" in the pot of Ninja Foodi Grill.
4. Close the Ninja Foodi Grill with lid and select "Air Crisp".
5. Set the temperature to 390 degrees F to preheat.
6. Press "Start/Stop" to begin preheating.
7. When the display shows "Add Food" open the lid and place the shrimp in the "Crisper Basket" in a single layer.
8. Close the Ninja Foodi Grill with lid and set the time for 7 minutes.
9. Press "Start/Stop" to begin cooking.
10. When cooking time is completed, press "Start/Stop" to stop cooking and open the lid.
11. Serve warm.

Serving Suggestions: These shrimp will be great with any kind of dipping sauce

Variation Tip: Pat dry the shrimp before wrapping.

Nutritional Information per Serving:

Calories: 499 | **Fat:** 32.9g|**Sat Fat:** 10.8g|**Carbohydrates:** 2.2g|**Fiber:** 0g|**Sugar:** 0g|**Protein:** 42.5g

Mozzarella Flatbread

Preparation Time: 10 minutes
Cooking Time: 5 minutes
Servings: 10

Ingredients:

- 1 tube prepared pizza dough
- ½ cup butter
- 1 teaspoon garlic
- Pinch of dried parsley
- 2 cups mozzarella cheese, shredded

Preparation:

1. Open and unroll the pizza dough.
2. From the long side, reroll the dough.
3. Cut 1-inch rolls from dough and then flatten each roll.
4. In a bowl, add the butter, garlic, and parsley and mix well.
5. Brush the top of dough with butter mixture.
6. Arrange the greased "Crisper Basket" in the pot of Ninja Foodi Grill.
7. Close the Ninja Foodi Grill with lid and select "Air Crisp".
8. Set the temperature to 350 degrees F to preheat.
9. Press "Start/Stop" to begin preheating.
10. When the display shows "Add Food" open the lid and place the rolls in the "Crisper Basket" in a single layer.
11. Close the Ninja Foodi Grill with lid and set the time for 5 minutes.
12. Press "Start/Stop" to begin cooking.
13. When cooking time is completed, press "Start/Stop" to stop cooking and open the lid.
14. Place the rolls onto a wire rack for about 5 minutes before serving.

Serving Suggestions: Serve with the drizzling of melted butter.

Variation Tip: You can top this bread with more fresh herbs.

Nutritional Information per Serving:

Calories: 126 | **Fat:** 12.1g|**Sat Fat:** 6.9g|**Carbohydrates:** 2.8g|**Fiber:** 0.2g| **Sugar:** 0g|**Protein:** 2.1g

Onion Dip

Preparation Time: 10 minutes
Cooking Time: 35 minutes
Servings: 8

Ingredients:

- 2/3 cup onion, chopped
- 1 cup cheddar Jack cheese, shredded
- ½ cup Swiss cheese, shredded
- ¼ cup Parmesan cheese, shredded
- 2/3 cup whipped salad dressing
- ½ cup milk
- Salt, to taste

Preparation:

1. In a large bowl, add all the ingredients and mix well.
2. Transfer the mixture into a baking pan and spread in an even layer.
3. Arrange the "Crisper Basket" in the pot of Ninja Foodi Grill.
4. Close the Ninja Foodi Grill with lid and select "Bake".
5. Set the temperature to 375 degrees F to preheat.
6. Press "Start/Stop" to begin preheating.
7. When the display shows "Add Food" open the lid and place the pan into the "Crisper Basket".
8. Close the Ninja Foodi Grill with lid and set the time for 45 minutes.
9. Press "Start/Stop" to begin cooking.
10. When cooking time is completed, press "Start/Stop" to stop cooking and open the lid.
11. Serve hot.

Serving Suggestions: Enjoy with tortilla chips.

Variation Tip: You can also add scallion greens in this dip.

Nutritional Information per Serving:

Calories: 108 | **Fat:** 7.5g | **Sat Fat:** 4.4g | **Carbohydrates:** 2.8g | **Fiber:** 0.3g | **Sugar:** 1.4g | **Protein:** 6.4g

Spinach Dip

Preparation Time: 15 minutes
Cooking Time: 35 minutes
Servings: 8

Ingredients:

- 1 (8-ounce) package cream cheese, softened
- 1 cup mayonnaise
- 1 cup Parmesan cheese, grated
- 1 cup frozen spinach, thawed and squeezed
- 1/3 cup water chestnuts, drained and chopped
- ½ cup onion, minced
- ¼ teaspoon garlic powder
- Freshly ground black pepper, to taste

Preparation:

1. In a bowl, add all the ingredients and mix until well combined.
2. Transfer the mixture into a baking pan and spread in an even layer.
3. Arrange the "Crisper Basket" in the pot of Ninja Foodi Grill.
4. Close the Ninja Foodi Grill with lid and select "Bake".
5. Set the temperature to 300 degrees F to preheat.
6. Press "Start/Stop" to begin preheating.
7. When the display shows "Add Food" open the lid and place the pan into the "Crisper Basket".
8. Close the Ninja Foodi Grill with lid and set the time for 30 minutes.
9. Press "Start/Stop" to begin cooking.
10. Stir the dip once halfway through.
11. When cooking time is completed, press "Start/Stop" to stop cooking and open the lid.
12. Serve hot.

Serving Suggestions: Enjou with fish crackers.

Variation Tip: use high-quality cream cheese.

Nutritional Information per Serving:

Calories: 258 | **Fat:** 22.1g | **Sat Fat:** 8.9g | **Carbohydrates:** 9.4g | **Fiber:** 0.3g | **Sugar:** 2.3g | **Protein:** 6.7g

Fish & Seafood Recipes

Zesty Salmon

Preparation Time: 10 minutes
Cooking Time: 8minutes
Servings: 4

Ingredients:

- 1½ pounds salmon fillets
- ½ teaspoon red chili powder
- Salt and freshly ground black pepper, to taste
- 1 lime, cut into slices
- 1 tablespoon fresh dill, chopped

Preparation:

1. Arrange the greased "Crisper Basket" in the pot of Ninja Foodi Grill.
2. Close the Ninja Foodi Grill with lid and select "Air Crisp".
3. Set the temperature to 375 degrees F to preheat.
4. Press "Start/Stop" to begin preheating.
5. Season the salmon with chili powder, salt, and black pepper evenly.
6. When the display shows "Add Food" open the lid and place the salmon fillets into the "Crisper Basket".
7. Close the Ninja Foodi Grill with lid and set the time for 8 minutes.
8. Press "Start/Stop" to begin cooking.
9. When cooking time is completed, press "Start/Stop" to stop cooking and open the lid.
10. Serve hot with the garnishing of dill.

Serving Suggestions: Enjoy with parsnip puree.

Variation Tip: You can use fresh parsley instrad of dill.

Nutritional Information per Serving:

Calories: 229 | **Fat:** 10.6g|**Sat Fat:** 1.5g|**Carbohydrates:** 1g|**Fiber:** 0.3g| **Sugar:** 0.1g|**Protein:** 33.2g

Glazed Salmon

Preparation Time: 10 minutes
Cooking Time: 13 minutes
Servings: 2

Ingredients:

- 3 tablespoons low-sodium soy sauce
- 2 tablespoons maple syrup
- 2 teaspoons fresh lemon juice
- 2 teaspoons water
- 2 (4-ounce) salmon fillets

Preparation:

1. Place all the ingredients in a small bowl except the salmon and mix well.
2. In a small bowl, reserve about half of the mixture.
3. Add the salmon in the remaining mixture and coat well.
4. Refrigerate, covered to marinate for about 2 hours.
5. Arrange the "Crisper Basket" in the pot of Ninja Foodi Grill.
6. Close the Ninja Foodi Grill with lid and select "Air Crisp".
7. Set the temperature to 355 degrees F to preheat.
8. Press "Start/Stop" to begin preheating.
9. When the display shows "Add Food" open the lid and place the salmon fillets into the "Crisper Basket" in a single layer.
10. Close the Ninja Foodi Grill with lid and set the time for 13 minutes.
11. Press "Start/Stop" to begin cooking.
12. After 8 minutes, flip the salmon fillets and coat with reserved marinade.
13. When the cooking time is completed, press "Start/Stop" to stop cooking and open the lid.
14. Serve hot.

Serving Suggestions: Enjoy with mashed potatoes.

Variation Tip: Salmon should look bright and shiny.

Nutritional Information per Serving:

Calories: 211 | **Fat:** 7.1g|**Sat Fat:** 1.1g|**Carbohydrates:** 15g|**Fiber:** 0g|**Sugar:** 13.5g|**Protein:** 23.5g

Teriyaki Salmon

Preparation Time: 10 minutes
Cooking Time: 8 minutes
Servings: 4

Ingredients:

- 4 (6-ounce) skinless salmon fillets
- 1 cup teriyaki marinade

Preparation:

1. In a bowl, place all the salmon fillets and teriyaki marinade and mix well.
2. Refrigerate, covered to marinate for about 2-3 hours.
3. Arrange the "Grill Grate" in the pot of Ninja Foodi Grill.
4. Close the Ninja Foodi Grill with lid and select "Grill" to "Max" to preheat.
5. Press "Start/Stop" to begin preheating.
6. When the display shows "Add Food" open the lid and place the salmon fillets onto the "Grill Grate".
7. With your hands, gently press down each fillet.
8. Close the Ninja Foodi Grill with lid and set the time for 8 minutes.
9. Press "Start/Stop" to begin cooking.
10. After 5 minutes of cooking, flip the salmon fillets.
11. When cooking time is completed, press "Start/Stop" to stop cooking and open the lid.
12. Serve hot.

Serving Suggestions: Serve with lemon butter.

Variation Tip: Dry the salmon fillets completely.

Nutritional Information per Serving:

Calories: 305 | **Fat:** 10.5g|**Sat Fat:** 1.5g|**Carbohydrates:** 16g|**Fiber:** 0g|**Sugar:** 12g|**Protein:** 33g

Glazed Haddock

Preparation Time: 10 minutes
Cooking Time: 15 minutes
Servings: 4

Ingredients:

- 1 garlic clove, minced
- ¼ teaspoon fresh ginger, grated finely
- ½ cup low-sodium soy sauce
- ¼ cup fresh orange juice
- 2 tablespoons fresh lime juice
- ½ cup cooking wine
- ¼ cup sugar
- ¼ teaspoon red pepper flakes, crushed
- 1 pound haddock steaks

Preparation:

1. In a pan, add all the ingredients except haddock steaks and bring to a boil.
2. Cook for about 3-4 minutes, stirring continuously.
3. Remove from the heat and set aside to cool.
4. In a reseal able bag, add half of marinade and haddock steaks.
5. Seal the bag and shake to coat well.
6. Refrigerate for about 30 minutes.
7. Remove the fish steaks from bag, reserving the remaining marinade.
8. Arrange the greased "Crisper Basket" in the pot of Ninja Foodi Grill.
9. Close the Ninja Foodi Grill with lid and select "Air Crisp".
10. Set the temperature to 390 degrees F to preheat.
11. Press "Start/Stop" to begin preheating.
12. When the display shows "Add Food" open the lid and place the haddock steaks into the "Crisper Basket".
13. Close the Ninja Foodi Grill with lid and set the time for 11 minutes.
14. Press "Start/Stop" to begin cooking.
15. When the cooking time is completed, press "Start/Stop" to stop cooking and open the lid.
16. Transfer the haddock steak onto a serving platter.
17. Immediately, coat the haddock steak with the remaining glaze and serve.

Serving Suggestions: Serve with steamed green beans.

Variation Tip: Use freshly squeezed orange juice.

Nutritional Information per Serving:

Calories: 218 | **Fat:** 1.1g | **Sat Fat:** 0.2g | **Carbohydrates:** 17.4g | **Fiber:** 0.1g | **Sugar:** 16.1g | **Protein:** 129.7g

Buttered Halibut

Preparation Time: 10 minutes
Cooking Time: 30 minutes
Servings: 4

Ingredients:

- 1 pound halibut fillets
- 1 tablespoon ginger paste
- 1 tablespoon garlic paste
- Salt and freshly ground black pepper, to taste
- 3 jalapeño peppers, chopped
- ¾ cup butter, chopped

Preparation:

1. Arrange the "Crisper Basket" in the pot of Ninja Foodi Grill.
2. Close the Ninja Foodi Grill with lid and select "Roast".
3. Set the temperature to 380 degrees F to preheat.
4. Press "Start/Stop" to begin preheating.
5. Coat the halibut fillets with ginger-garlic paste and then season with salt and black pepper.
6. When the display shows "Add Food" open the lid and place the halibut fillets into the "Crisper Basket" in a single layer and top with jalapeño peppers, followed by the butter.
7. Close the Ninja Foodi Grill with lid and set the time for 30 minutes.
8. Press "Start/Stop" to begin cooking.
9. When the cooking time is completed, press "Start/Stop" to stop cooking and open the lid.
10. Serve hot.

Serving Suggestions: Fresh baby greens will be great if served with this fish.

Variation Tip: You can adjust the quantity of jalapeño according to your taste.

Nutritional Information per Serving:

Calories: 355 | **Fat:** 29.9g|**Sat Fat:** 17.8g|**Carbohydrates:** 2g|**Fiber:** 0.5g|**Sugar:** 0.4g|**Protein:** 19.7g

Spiced Tilapia

Preparation Time: 10 minutes
Cooking Time: 12 minutes
Servings: 2

Ingredients:

- ½ teaspoon lemon pepper seasoning
- ½ teaspoon garlic powder
- 1/2 teaspoon onion powder
- Salt and freshly ground black pepper, to taste
- 2 (6-ounce) tilapia fillets
- 1 tablespoon olive oil

Preparation:

1. In a small bowl, mix together the spices, salt and black pepper.
2. Coat the tilapia fillets with oil and then rub with spice mixture.
3. Arrange the greased "Crisper Basket" in the pot of Ninja Foodi Grill.
4. Close the Ninja Foodi Grill with lid and select "Air Crisp".
5. Set the temperature to 360 degrees F to preheat.
6. Press "Start/Stop" to begin preheating.
7. When the display shows "Add Food" open the lid and place the tilapia fillets into the "Crisper Basket".
8. Close the Ninja Foodi Grill with lid and set the time for 12 minutes.
9. Press "Start/Stop" to begin cooking.
10. Flip the fillets once halfway through.
11. When the cooking time is completed, press "Start/Stop" to stop cooking and open the lid.
12. Serve hot.

Serving Suggestions: Serve with the drizzling of lime juice.

Variation Tip: You can use fresh garlic instead of garlic powder.

Nutritional Information per Serving:

Calories: 206 | **Fat:** 8.6g | **Sat Fat:** 1.6g | **Carbohydrates:** 0.2g | **Fiber:** 0.1g | **Sugar:** 0.4g | **Protein:** 31.9g

Parmesan Shrimp

Preparation Time: 15 minutes
Cooking Time: 20 minutes
Servings: 4

Ingredients:

- 2/3 cup Parmesan cheese, grated
- 4 garlic cloves, minced
- 2 tablespoons olive oil
- 1 teaspoon dried basil
- ½ teaspoon dried oregano
- 1 teaspoon onion powder
- ½ teaspoon red pepper flakes, crushed
- Freshly ground black pepper, to taste
- 2 pounds shrimp, peeled and deveined
- 1-2 tablespoons fresh lemon juice

Preparation:

1. Arrange the greased "Crisper Basket" in the pot of Ninja Foodi Grill.
2. Close the Ninja Foodi Grill with lid and select "Air Crisp".
3. Set the temperature to 350 degrees F to preheat.
4. Press "Start/Stop" to begin preheating.
5. In a large bowl, add the Parmesan cheese, garlic, oil, herbs, and spices and mix well.
6. Add the shrimp and toss to coat well.
7. When the display shows "Add Food" open the lid and place half of the shrimp into the "Crisper Basket" in a single layer.
8. Close the Ninja Foodi Grill with lid and set the time for 10 minutes.
9. Press "Start/Stop" to begin cooking.
10. When cooking time is completed, press "Start/Stop" to stop cooking and open the lid.
11. Transfer the shrimp onto a platter.
12. Repeat with the remaining shrimp.
13. Drizzle with lemon juice and serve immediately.

Serving Suggestions: Serve with the garnishing of parsley.

Variation Tip: Avoid shrimp that smell like ammonia.

Nutritional Information per Serving:

Calories: 386 | **Fat:** 14.2g|**Sat Fat:** 3.8g|**Carbohydrates:** 5.3g|**Fiber:** 0.3g|**Sugar:** 0.4g|**Protein:** 57.3g

Shrimp Kabobs

Preparation Time: 15 minutes
Cooking Time: 8 minutes
Servings: 2

Ingredients:

- ¾ pound shrimp, peeled and deveined
- 2 tablespoons fresh lemon juice
- 1 teaspoon garlic, minced
- ½ teaspoon paprika
- ½ teaspoon ground cumin
- Salt and freshly ground black pepper, to taste
- 1 tablespoon fresh cilantro, chopped

Preparation:

1. In a bowl, mix together the lemon juice, garlic, and spices.
2. Add the shrimp and mix well.
3. Thread the shrimp onto presoaked wooden skewers.
4. Arrange the greased "Crisper Basket" in the pot of Ninja Foodi Grill.
5. Close the Ninja Foodi Grill with lid and select "Air Crisp".
6. Set the temperature to 350 degrees F to preheat.
7. Press "Start/Stop" to begin preheating.
8. When the display shows "Add Food" open the lid and place the shrimp skewers into the "Crisper Basket".
9. Close the Ninja Foodi Grill with lid and set the time for 8 minutes.
10. Press "Start/Stop" to begin cooking.
11. Flip the shrimp kabobs once halfway through.
12. When cooking time is completed, press "Start/Stop" to stop cooking and open the lid.
13. Transfer the shrimp kabobs onto serving plates.
14. Garnish with fresh cilantro and serve immediately.

Serving Suggestions: Serve with fresh salad.

Variation Tip: Use equal-sized shrimp in yhis recipe

Nutritional Information per Serving:

Calories: 212 | **Fat:** 3.2g | **Sat Fat:** 1.2g | **Carbohydrates:** 3.9g | **Fiber:** 0.4g | **Sugar:** 0.4g | **Protein:** 39.1g

Shrimp Scampi

Preparation Time: 15 minutes
Cooking Time: 5 minutes
Servings: 3

Ingredients:

- 4 tablespoons salted butter
- 1 tablespoon fresh lemon juice
- 1 tablespoon garlic, minced
- 2 teaspoons red pepper flakes, crushed
- 1 pound shrimp, peeled and deveined
- 2 tablespoons fresh basil, chopped
- 1 tablespoon fresh chives, chopped
- 2 tablespoons chicken broth

Preparation:

1. Arrange a 7-inch round baking pan in the "Crisper Basket".
2. Now, arrange the "Crisper Basket" in the pot of Ninja Foodi Grill.
3. Close the Ninja Foodi Grill with lid and select "Air Crisp".
4. Set the temperature to 325 degrees F to preheat.
5. Press "Start/Stop" to begin preheating.
6. When the display shows "Add Food" open the lid and carefully remove the pan from Ninja Foodi.
7. In the heated pan, place the butter, lemon juice, garlic, and red pepper flakes and mix well.
8. Place the pan into the "Crisper Basket".
9. Close the Ninja Foodi Grill with lid and set the time for 7 minutes.
10. Press "Start/Stop" to begin cooking.
11. After 2 minutes of cooking, stir in the shrimp, basil, chives and broth.
12. When cooking time is completed, press "Start/Stop" to stop cooking and open the lid
13. Place the pan onto a wire rack for about 1 minute.
14. Stir the mixture and serve hot.

Serving Suggestions: Serve with crusty bread.

Variation Tip: You can also use fish broth in this recipe.

Nutritional Information per Serving:

Calories: 245 | **Fat:** 15.7g | **Sat Fat:** 8g | **Carbohydrates:** 3.1g | **Fiber:** 0.3g | **Sugar:** 0.2g | **Protein:** 26.4g

Rosemary Scallops

Preparation Time: 15 minutes
Cooking Time: 6 minutes
Servings: 6

Ingredients:

- ½ cup butter
- 4 garlic cloves, minced
- 1 tablespoon fresh rosemary, chopped
- 1 tablespoon fresh thyme, chopped
- 2 pounds sea scallops
- Salt and freshly ground black pepper, to taste

Preparation:

1. In a skillet, melt the butter over medium heat and sauté the garlic and rosemary for about 1 minute.
2. Stir in the scallops, salt and black pepper and cook for about 2 minutes.
3. Remove from the heat and place the scallop mixture into a baking pan.
4. Arrange the "Crisper Basket" in the pot of Ninja Foodi Grill.
5. Close the Ninja Foodi Grill with lid and select "Air Crisp".
6. Set the temperature to 350 degrees F to preheat.
7. Press "Start/Stop" to begin preheating.
8. When the display shows "Add Food" open the lid and place the pan into the "Crisper Basket".
9. Close the Ninja Foodi Grill with lid and set the time for 3 minutes.
10. Press "Start/Stop" to begin cooking.
11. When cooking time is completed, press "Start/Stop" to stop cooking and open the lid.
12. Serve hot.

Serving Suggestions: Serve with fresh green salad.

Variation Tip: Use unsalted butter.

Nutritional Information per Serving:

Calories: 275 | **Fat:** 16.6g|**Sat Fat:** 9.8g|**Carbohydrates:** 4.9g|**Fiber:** 0.4g| **Sugar:** 0g|**Protein:** 25.7g

Scallops in Capers Sauce

Preparation Time: 15 minutes
Cooking Time: 6 minutes
Servings: 3

Ingredients:

- 12 (1-ounce) sea scallops, cleaned and patted very dry
- Salt and freshly ground black pepper, to taste
- ¼ cup olive oil
- 2 tablespoons fresh parsley, finely chopped
- 2 teaspoons capers, finely chopped
- 1 teaspoon fresh lemon zest, finely grated
- ½ teaspoon garlic, finely chopped

Preparation:

1. Arrange the greased "Crisper Basket" in the pot of Ninja Foodi Grill.
2. Close the Ninja Foodi Grill with lid and select "Air Crisp".
3. Set the temperature to 400 degrees F to preheat.
4. Press "Start/Stop" to begin preheating.
5. Season each scallop with salt and black pepper evenly.
6. When the display shows "Add Food" open the lid and place the scallops into the "Crisper Basket".
7. Close the Ninja Foodi Grill with lid and set the time for 6 minutes.
8. Press "Start/Stop" to begin cooking.
9. Meanwhile, for sauce: in a bowl, mix the remaining ingredients.
10. When cooking time is completed, press "Start/Stop" to stop cooking and open the lid
11. Transfer the scallops onto serving plates.
12. Top with the sauce and serve immediately.

Serving Suggestions: Serve with the topping of freshly grated Parmesan.

Variation Tip: Scallops should smell sea fresh.

Nutritional Information per Serving:

Calories: 246 | **Fat:** 17.7g | **Sat Fat:** 2.5g | **Carbohydrates:** 3.2g | **Fiber:** 0.2g | **Sugar:** 0.1g | **Protein:** 19.2g

Glazed Calamari

Preparation Time: 15 minutes
Cooking Time: 13 minutes
Servings: 3

Ingredients:

- ¾ pound calamari tubes, washed and cut into ¼-inch rings
- 1 cup club soda
- 1 cup flour
- ½ tablespoon red pepper flakes, crushed
- Salt and freshly ground black pepper, to taste
- 2 tablespoons Sriracha
- ½ cup honey
- Olive oil cooking spray

Preparation:

1. In a large bowl, place the calamari and club soda and set aside for about 10 minutes.
2. Meanwhile, in a shallow bowl, place the flour, red pepper flakes, salt and black pepper and mix well.
3. Drain the club soda from the calamari.
4. With the paper towels, pat dry the calamari rings.
5. Coat the calamari rings with flour mixture evenly.
6. Arrange the greased "Crisper Basket" in the pot of Ninja Foodi Grill.
7. Close the Ninja Foodi Grill with lid and select "Air Crisp".
8. Set the temperature to 375 degrees F to preheat.
9. Press "Start/Stop" to begin preheating.
10. When the display shows "Add Food" open the lid and place the calamari rings into the "Crisper Basket".
11. Close the Ninja Foodi Grill with lid and set the time for 13 minutes.
12. Press "Start/Stop" to begin cooking.
13. While cooking, shake the "Crisper Basket" occasionally.
14. Meanwhile, in a bowl, place the Sriracha and honey and beat until well combined.
15. After 11 minutes, coat the calamari rings with honey mixture evenly.
16. When cooking time is completed, press "Start/Stop" to stop cooking and open the lid.
17. Serve hot.

Serving Suggestions: Garnish with fresh herbs before serving.

Variation Tip: Wrinkled or smells calamari should be avoided.

Nutritional Information per Serving:

Calories: 443 | **Fat:** 4.6g | **Sat Fat:** 0.6g | **Carbohydrates:** 89g | **Fiber:** 2g | **Sugar:** 46g | **Protein:** 12.6g

Poultry Mains Recipes

Roasted Cornish Hen

Preparation Time: 15 minutes
Cooking Time: 40 minutes
Servings: 4

Ingredients:

- 1 teaspoon dried rosemary, crushed
- 1 teaspoon dried thyme, crushed
- 1 teaspoon poultry seasoning
- 1 teaspoon garlic powder
- 1 teaspoon smoked paprika
- Salt and freshly ground black pepper, to taste
- 2 (1¼-pound) Cornish hens
- 2-3 tablespoons olive oil
- 1 lemon, cut into slices

Preparation:

1. In a small bowl, mix together the dried herbs, poultry seasoning, spices, salt and black pepper.
2. Brush both hens with oil and then sprinkle with herb mixture evenly.
3. Arrange the greased "Crisper Basket" in the pot of Ninja Foodi Grill.
4. Close the Ninja Foodi Grill with lid and select "Air Crisp".
5. Set the temperature to 350 degrees F to preheat.
6. Press "Start/Stop" to begin preheating.
7. When the display shows "Add Food" open the lid and place the lemon slices into the "Crisper Basket".
8. Arrange both hens over lemon slices.
9. Close the Ninja Foodi Grill with lid and set the time for 40 minutes.
10. Press "Start/Stop" to begin cooking.
11. Flip the hens once after 20 minutes.
12. When cooking time is completed, press "Start/Stop" to stop cooking and open the lid.
13. Place the hens onto a cutting board for about 15 minutes.
14. Cut each hen into desired sized pieces and serve.

Serving Suggestions: Roasted vegetables will accompany nicely.

Variation Tip: Adjust the ratio of herbs according to your taste.

Nutritional Information per Serving:

Calories: 448 | **Fat:** 18.2g | **Sat Fat:** 3.9g | **Carbohydrates:** 1.8g | **Fiber:** 0.6g | **Sugar:** 0.3g | **Protein:** 66.4g

Roasted Chicken with Potatoes

Preparation Time: 10 minutes
Cooking Time: 1 hour
Servings: 2

Ingredients:

- 1 (1½-pound) whole chicken
- Salt and freshly ground black pepper, to taste
- 1 tablespoon dried rosemary, crushed
- ½ pound small potatoes
- 1 tablespoon olive oil

Preparation:

1. Arrange the greased "Crisper Basket" in the pot of Ninja Foodi Grill.
2. Close the Ninja Foodi Grill with lid and select "Air Crisp".
3. Set the temperature to 390 degrees F to preheat.
4. Press "Start/Stop" to begin preheating.
5. Season the chicken with salt and black pepper and then rub with rosemary.
6. When the display shows "Add Food" open the lid and place the chicken into the "Crisper Basket".
7. Close the Ninja Foodi Grill with lid and set the time for 60 minutes.
8. Press "Start/Stop" to begin cooking.
9. Meanwhile, in a bowl, add the potatoes, oil, salt and black pepper and toss to coat well.
10. After 40 minutes of cooking, arrange the potatoes into the "Crisper Basket".
11. When the cooking time is completed, press "Start/Stop" to stop cooking and open the lid.
12. Place the chicken onto a cutting board for about 10 minutes.
13. Cut the chicken into desired sized pieces and serve alongside the potatoes.

Serving Suggestions: Serve wit the drizzling of lemon juice.

Variation Tip: You can also add carrot chunks alongside the potatoes.

Nutritional Information per Serving:

Calories: 624 | **Fat:** 37.4g | **Sat Fat:** 10.2g | **Carbohydrates:** 18.9g | **Fiber:** 3.4g | **Sugar:** 1.3g | **Protein:** 59g

Spicy Roasted Chicken

Preparation Time: 15 minutes
Cooking Time: 1 hour
Servings: 6

Ingredients:

- 2 teaspoons dried thyme
- 2 teaspoons paprika
- 1 teaspoon cayenne pepper
- 1 teaspoon ground white pepper
- 1 teaspoon onion powder
- 1 teaspoon garlic powder
- 1 (5-pound) whole chicken, necks and giblets removed
- 3 tablespoons oil
- Salt and freshly ground black pepper, to taste

Preparation:

1. In a bowl, mix together the thyme and spices.
2. Coat the chicken with oil and then rub it with spice mixture.
3. Season the chicken with salt and black pepper evenly.
4. Arrange the greased "Crisper Basket" in the pot of Ninja Foodi Grill.
5. Close the Ninja Foodi Grill with lid and select "Air Crisp".
6. Set the temperature to 350 degrees F to preheat.
7. Press "Start/Stop" to begin preheating.
8. When the display shows "Add Food" open the lid and place the chicken into the "Crisper Basket".
9. Close the Ninja Foodi Grill with lid and set the time for 1 hour.
10. Press "Start/Stop" to begin cooking.
11. Flip the chicken once after 30 minutes.
12. When cooking time is completed, press "Start/Stop" to stop cooking and open the lid.
13. Place the chicken onto a cutting board for about 10 minutes before carving.
14. Cut the chicken into desired sized pieces and serve.

Serving Suggestions: steamed veggies will go great wit this chicken.

Variation Tip: Adjust the ratio of spices according to your choice.

Nutritional Information per Serving:

Calories: 601 | **Fat:** 40.5g|**Sat Fat:** 11g|**Carbohydrates:** 1.7g|**Fiber:** 0.6g|**Sugar:** 0.4g|**Protein:** 63.7g

Sweet & Spicy Chicken Drumsticks

Preparation Time: 10 minutes
Cooking Time: 20 minutes
Servings: 4

Ingredients:

- 1 garlic clove, crushed
- 1 teaspoon cayenne pepper
- 1 teaspoon red chili powder
- 2 teaspoons sugar
- 1 tablespoon mustard
- Salt and freshly ground black pepper, to taste
- 1 tablespoon olive oil
- 4 (6-ounce) chicken drumsticks

Preparation:

1. In a bowl, mix together all ingredients except chicken drumsticks.
2. Rub the chicken with the oil mix and refrigerate to marinate for about 20-30 minutes.
3. Arrange the greased "Crisper Basket" in the pot of Ninja Foodi Grill.
4. Close the Ninja Foodi Grill with lid and select "Air Crisp".
5. Set the temperature to 390 degrees F to preheat.
6. Press "Start/Stop" to begin preheating.
7. When the display shows "Add Food" open the lid and place the chicken drumsticks into the "Crisper Basket".
8. Close the Ninja Foodi Grill with lid and set the time for 10 minutes.
9. Press "Start/Stop" to begin cooking.
10. After 10 minutes of cooking, set the temperature to 300 degrees F for 10 minutes.
11. When cooking time is completed, press "Start/Stop" to stop cooking and open the lid.
12. Serve hot.

Serving Suggestions: Enjoy with your favorite dipping sauce.

Variation Tip: Select the chicken legs with a pinkish hue.

Nutritional Information per Serving:

Calories: 343 | **Fat:** 14.2g|**Sat Fat:** 3.1g|**Carbohydrates:** 3.8g|**Fiber:** 0.8g|**Sugar:** 2.3g|**Protein:** 47.7g

BBQ Chicken Breasts

Preparation Time: 10 minutes
Cooking Time: 22 minutes
Servings: 4

Ingredients:

- 4 (8-ounce) frozen boneless, skinless chicken breasts
- 2 tablespoons olive oil, divided
- Salt and ground black pepper, as required
- 1 cup BBQ sauce

Preparation:

1. Brush the chicken breasts with ½ tablespoon of oil evenly and season with salt and black pepper.
2. Arrange the greased "Crisper Basket" in the pot of Ninja Foodi Grill.
3. Close the Ninja Foodi Grill with lid and select "Broil" to preheat.
4. Press "Start/Stop" to begin preheating.
5. When the display shows "Add Food" open the lid and place the chicken breasts into the "Crisper Basket".
6. Close the Ninja Foodi Grill with lid and set the time for 22 minutes.
7. Press "Start/Stop" to begin cooking.
8. After 10 minutes of cooking, flip the chicken breasts.
9. After 15 minutes of cooking, flip the chicken breasts and coat the upper side with barbecue sauce generously.
10. After 20 minutes of cooking, flip the chicken breasts and coat the upper side with barbecue sauce generously.
11. When the cooking time is completed, press "Start/Stop" to stop cooking and open the lid.
12. Place the chicken breasts onto a platter and set aside for about 5 minutes before serving.

Serving Suggestions: Serve with maple glazed carrots.

Variation Tip: Try to pick a package with breasts of similar size.

Nutritional Information per Serving:

Calories: 585 | **Fat:** 24g | **Sat Fat:** 5.6g | **Carbohydrates:** 22.7g | **Fiber:** 0.4g | **Sugar:** 10g | **Protein:** 65.6g

Sausage Stuffed Chicken Breast

Preparation Time: 15 minutes
Cooking Time: 15 minutes
Servings: 4

Ingredients:

- 4 (4-ounce) skinless, boneless chicken breasts
- 4 sausage links, casing removed

Preparation:

1. With a rolling pin, roll each chicken breast for about 1 minute.
2. Arrange the chicken breasts onto a smooth surface.
3. Place 1 sausage over each chicken breast.
4. Roll each breast around the sausage and secure with toothpicks.
5. Arrange the greased "Crisper Basket" in the pot of Ninja Foodi Grill.
6. Close the Ninja Foodi Grill with lid and select "Air Crisp".
7. Set the temperature to 375 degrees F to preheat.
8. Press "Start/Stop" to begin preheating.
9. When the display shows "Add Food" open the lid and place the chicken breasts into the "Crisper Basket".
10. Close the Ninja Foodi Grill with lid and set the time for 15 minutes.
11. Press "Start/Stop" to begin cooking.
12. When cooking time is completed, press "Start/Stop" to stop cooking and open the lid.
13. Serve hot.

Serving Suggestions: Serve with the garnishing of cheese.

Variation Tip: You can use any kind of sausage for stuffing.

Nutritional Information per Serving:

Calories: 423 | **Fat:** 27.6g|**Sat Fat:** 9.1g|**Carbohydrates:** 0g|**Fiber:** 0g|**Sugar:** 0g|**Protein:** 41.4g

Spinach Stuffed Chicken Breasts

Preparation Time: 15 minutes
Cooking Time: 30 minutes
Servings: 2

Ingredients:

- 1 tablespoon olive oil
- 1¾ ounces fresh spinach
- ¼ cup ricotta cheese, shredded
- 2 (4-ounce) skinless, boneless chicken breasts
- Salt and freshly ground black pepper, to taste
- 2 tablespoons cheddar cheese, grated
- ¼ teaspoon paprika

Preparation:

1. In a skillet, heat the oil over medium heat and cook the spinach for about 3-4 minutes.
2. Stir in the ricotta and cook for about 40-60 seconds.
3. Remove from heat and transfer the spinach mixture into a bowl. Set aside to cool.
4. Cut slits into the chicken breasts about ¼-inch apart but not all the way through.
5. Stuff each chicken breast with the spinach mixture.
6. Sprinkle each chicken breast with salt and black pepper and then with cheddar cheese and paprika.
7. Arrange the greased "Crisper Basket" in the pot of Ninja Foodi Grill.
8. Close the Ninja Foodi Grill with lid and select "Air Crisp".
9. Set the temperature to 390 degrees F to preheat.
10. Press "Start/Stop" to begin preheating.
11. When the display shows "Add Food" open the lid and place the chicken breasts into the "Crisper Basket".
12. Close the Ninja Foodi Grill with lid and set the time for 25 minutes.
13. Press "Start/Stop" to begin cooking.
14. When cooking time is completed, press "Start/Stop" to stop cooking and open the lid.
15. Serve hot.

Serving Suggestions: Buttery mashed potatoes will go great with these stuffed chicken breasts.

Variation Tip: Avoid overcooking of chicken breasts.

Nutritional Information per Serving:

Calories: 279 | **Fat:** 16g | **Sat Fat:** 5.6g | **Carbohydrates:** 2.7g | **Fiber:** 0.7g | **Sugar:** 0.3g | **Protein:** 31.4g

Buttermilk Brined Turkey Breast

Preparation Time: 15 minutes
Cooking Time: 25 minutes
Servings: 8

Ingredients:

- ¾ cup brine from a can of olives
- ½ cup buttermilk
- 3½ pounds boneless, skinless turkey breast
- 2 fresh thyme sprigs
- 1 fresh rosemary sprig

Preparation:

1. In a bowl, add the olive brine and buttermilk and beat until well combined.
2. In a resealable plastic bag, place the turkey breast, buttermilk mixture and herb sprigs.
3. Seal the bag and refrigerate for about 8 hours.
4. Remove the turkey breast from bag and set aside until it reaches room temperature.
5. Arrange the greased "Crisper Basket" in the pot of Ninja Foodi Grill.
6. Close the Ninja Foodi Grill with lid and select "Air Crisp".
7. Set the temperature to 350 degrees F to preheat.
8. Press "Start/Stop" to begin preheating.
9. When the display shows "Add Food" open the lid and place the turkey breasts into the "Crisper Basket".
10. Close the Ninja Foodi Grill with lid and set the time for 20-25 minutes.
11. Press "Start/Stop" to begin cooking.
12. Flip the turkey breast once after 15 minutes.
13. When cooking time is completed, press "Start/Stop" to stop cooking and open the lid.
14. Place the turkey breast onto a platter.
15. Cover the turkey breast loosely with a piece of foil for about 10-15 minutes before slicing.
16. Cut the turkey breast into desired sized slices and serve.

Serving Suggestions: Serve with fresh veggie salad.

Variation Tip: Avoid the turkey breast with flat spots.

Nutritional Information per Serving:

Calories: 238| **Fat:** 1.2g|**Sat Fat:** 0.2g|**Carbohydrates:** 1.7g|**Fiber:** 0.6g| **Sugar:** 0.7g|**Protein:** 49.6g

Buttered Turkey Breast

Preparation Time: 10 minutes
Cooking Time: 55 minutes
Servings: 6

Ingredients:

- ¼ cup butter, softened
- 4 tablespoons fresh rosemary, chopped
- Salt and freshly ground black pepper, to taste
- 1 (4-pound) bone-in, skin-on turkey breast
- 2 tablespoons olive oil

Preparation:

1. In a bowl, add the butter, rosemary, salt and black pepper and mix well.
2. Rub the herb mixture under skin evenly.
3. Coat the outside of turkey breast with oil.
4. Place the turkey breast into the greased baking pan.
5. Arrange the "Crisper Basket" in the pot of Ninja Foodi Grill.
6. Close the Ninja Foodi Grill with lid and select "Bake".
7. Set the temperature to 350 degrees F to preheat.
8. Press "Start/Stop" to begin preheating.
9. When the display shows "Add Food" open the lid and place the pan into the "Crisper Basket".
10. Close the Ninja Foodi Grill with lid and set the time for 55 minutes.
11. Press "Start/Stop" to begin cooking.
12. When cooking time is completed, press "Start/Stop" to stop cooking and open the lid.
13. Place the turkey breast onto a platter.
14. Cover the turkey breast loosely with a piece of foil for about 10-15 minutes before slicing.
15. Cut the turkey into desired sized slices and serve.

Serving Suggestions: Serve with the garnishing of lime.

Variation Tip: slice the breast crosswise into slices.

Nutritional Information per Serving:

Calories: 628 | **Fat:** 34.3g | **Sat Fat:** 11.1g | **Carbohydrates:** 1.4g | **Fiber:** 0.1g | **Sugar:** 0g | **Protein:** 65g

Thyme Turkey Tenderloins

Preparation Time: 10 minutes
Cooking Time: 20 minutes
Servings: 4

Ingredients:

- 1 teaspoon dried thyme, crushed
- 1 teaspoon garlic powder
- Salt and freshly ground black pepper, to taste
- 1 (24-ounce) package boneless turkey breast tenderloins
- 2 tablespoon olive oil

Preparation:

1. In a small bowl, mix together the thyme, garlic powder, salt and black pepper.
2. Rub the turkey tenderloins with thyme mixture evenly.
3. In a skillet, heat the oil over medium heat and cook the turkey tenderloins for about 10 minutes or until golden brown.
4. Remove from the heat and transfer the turkey tenderloins onto a plate.
5. Arrange the "Crisper Basket" in the pot of Ninja Foodi Grill.
6. Close the Ninja Foodi Grill with lid and select "Bake".
7. Set the temperature to 350 degrees F to preheat.
8. Press "Start/Stop" to begin preheating.
9. When the display shows "Add Food" open the lid and place the turkey tenderloins into the "Crisper Basket".
10. Close the Ninja Foodi Grill with lid and set the time for 10 minutes.
11. Press "Start/Stop" to begin cooking.
12. When cooking time is completed, press "Start/Stop" to stop cooking and open the lid.
13. Place the turkey tenderloins onto a cutting board for about 5 minutes before slicing.
14. Cut into desired sized slices and serve.

Serving Suggestions: Serve with the topping of fresh herbs.

Variation Tip: Make sure your turkey breast tenderloins are thawed before cooking.

Nutritional Information per Serving:

Calories: 244 | **Fat:** 9.2g | **Sat Fat:** 1.7g | **Carbohydrates:** 0.7g | **Fiber:** 0.2g | **Sugar:** 0.2g | **Protein:** 39.3g

Turkey Roll

Preparation Time: 15 minutes
Cooking Time: 40 minutes
Servings: 3

Ingredients:

- 1 pound turkey breast fillet
- 1 garlic clove, crushed
- 1½ teaspoons ground cumin
- 1 teaspoon ground cinnamon
- ½ teaspoon red chili powder
- Salt, to taste
- 2 tablespoons olive oil
- 3 tablespoons fresh parsley, chopped finely
- 1 small red onion, chopped finely

Preparation:

1. Place the turkey fillet on a cutting board.
2. Carefully cut horizontally along the length about 1/3 of way from the top, stopping about ¼-inch from the edge.
3. Open this part to have a long piece of fillet.
4. In a bowl, mix together the garlic, spices and oil.
5. In a small cup, reserve about 1 tablespoon of oil mixture.
6. In the remaining oil mixture, add the parsley and onion and mix well.
7. Coat the open side of fillet with onion mixture.
8. Roll the fillet tightly from the short side.
9. With a kitchen string, tie the roll at 1-1½-inch intervals.
10. Coat the outer side of roll with the reserved oil mixture.
11. Arrange the "Crisper Basket" in the pot of Ninja Foodi Grill.
12. Close the Ninja Foodi Grill with lid and select "Air Crisp".
13. Set the temperature to 355 degrees F to preheat.
14. Press "Start/Stop" to begin preheating.
15. When the display shows "Add Food" open the lid and place the turkey roll into the "Crisper Basket".
16. Close the Ninja Foodi Grill with lid and set the time for 40 minutes.
17. Press "Start/Stop" to begin cooking.
18. When cooking time is completed, press "Start/Stop" to stop cooking and open the lid.
19. Transfer the turkey roll onto a cutting board for about 5-10 minutes before slicing.
20. With a sharp knife, cut the turkey roll into desired size slices and serve.

Serving Suggestions: Enjoy with your favorite dipping sauce.

Variation Tip: Adjust the ratio of spices according to your liking.

Nutritional Information per Serving:

Calories: 319 | **Fat:** 11.8g|**Sat Fat:** 2.1g|**Carbohydrates:** 4.2g|**Fiber:** 1.5g|**Sugar:** 1.3g|**Protein:** 50g

Turkey & Yogurt Casserole

Preparation Time: 10 minutes
Cooking Time: 25 minutes
Servings: 4

Ingredients:

- 6 eggs
- ½ cup plain Greek yogurt
- ½ cup cooked turkey meat, chopped
- Salt and freshly ground black pepper, to taste
- ½ cup sharp Cheddar cheese, shredded

Preparation:

1. In a bowl, add the egg and yogurt and beat well.
2. Add the remaining ingredients and stir to combine.
3. In a greased baking pan, place the egg mixture.
4. Arrange the "Crisper Basket" in the pot of Ninja Foodi Grill.
5. Close the Ninja Foodi Grill with lid and select "Bake".
6. Set the temperature to 375 degrees F to preheat.
7. Press "Start/Stop" to begin preheating.
8. When the display shows "Add Food" open the lid and place the pan into the "Crisper Basket".
9. Close the Ninja Foodi Grill with lid and set the time for 25 minutes.
10. Press "Start/Stop" to begin cooking.
11. When cooking time is completed, press "Start/Stop" to stop cooking and open the lid.
12. Serve warm.

Serving Suggestions: Serve with your favorite salad.

Variation Tip: Make sure to use plain yogurt.

Nutritional Information per Serving:

Calories: 203 | **Fat:** 12.5g | **Sat Fat:** 5.6g | **Carbohydrates:** 2.9g | **Fiber:** 0g | **Sugar:** 2.7g | **Protein:** 18.7g

Turkey Meatloaf

Preparation Time: 20 minutes
Cooking Time: 20 minutes
Servings: 4

Ingredients:

- 1 pound ground turkey
- 1 cup fresh kale leaves, trimmed and finely chopped
- 1 cup onion, chopped
- 1 (4-ounces) can chopped green chilies
- 2 garlic cloves, minced
- 1 egg, beaten
- ½ cup fresh breadcrumbs
- 1 cup Monterey Jack cheese, grated
- ¼ cup salsa verde

- 3 tablespoons fresh cilantro, chopped
- 1 teaspoon red chili powder
- ½ teaspoon ground cumin
- ½ teaspoon dried oregano, crushed
- Salt and freshly ground black pepper, to taste

Preparation:

1. In a deep bowl, place all the ingredients and with your hands, mix until well combined.
2. Divide the turkey mixture into 4 equal-sized portions and shape each into a mini loaf.
3. Arrange the greased "Crisper Basket" in the pot of Ninja Foodi Grill.
4. Close the Ninja Foodi Grill with lid and select "Air Crisp".
5. Set the temperature to 400 degrees F to preheat.
6. Press "Start/Stop" to begin preheating.
7. When the display shows "Add Food" open the lid and place the loaves into the "Crisper Basket".
8. Close the Ninja Foodi Grill with lid and set the time for 20 minutes.
9. Press "Start/Stop" to begin cooking.
10. When the cooking time is completed, press "Start/Stop" to stop cooking and open the lid.
11. Place the loaves onto plates for about 5 minutes before serving.

Serving Suggestions: Serve with Italian peas.

Variation Tip: Y If you want a gluten-free option, then use pork rinds instead of breadcrumbs.

Nutritional Information per Serving:

Calories: 517 | **Fat:** 24.7g | **Sat Fat:** 8.2g | **Carbohydrates:** 36g | **Fiber:** 10.1g | **Sugar:** 14.3g | **Protein:** 45.4g

Glazed Duck Breasts

Preparation Time: 10 minutes
Cooking Time: 20 minutes
Servings: 2

Ingredients:

- 1 (10½-ounce) duck breast
- 1 tablespoon wholegrain mustard
- 1 teaspoon honey
- 1 teaspoon balsamic vinegar
- Salt and freshly ground black pepper, to taste

Preparation:

1. Arrange the greased "Crisper Basket" in the pot of Ninja Foodi Grill.
2. Close the Ninja Foodi Grill with lid and select "Air Crisp".
3. Set the temperature to 365 degrees F to preheat.
4. Press "Start/Stop" to begin preheating.
5. When the display shows "Add Food" open the lid and place the duck breast, skin side up into the "Crisper Basket".
6. Close the Ninja Foodi Grill with lid and set the time for 20 minutes.
7. Press "Start/Stop" to begin cooking.
8. Meanwhile, in a bowl, mix together the remaining ingredients.
9. After 15 minutes of cooking, coat the duck breast with the honey mixture generously.
10. When cooking time is completed, press "Start/Stop" to stop cooking and open the lid.
11. Place the duck breast onto a cutting board.
12. Cut into 2 portions and serve hot.

Serving Suggestions: Serve with steamed veggies.

Variation Tip: You can use fresh lime juice instead of vinegar.

Nutritional Information per Serving:

Calories: 229 | **Fat:** 7.6g|**Sat Fat:** 0.1g|**Carbohydrates:** 4.9g|**Fiber:** 0.8g|**Sugar:** 3.3g|**Protein:** 34.2g

Sides & Vegetable Recipes

Stuffed Tomatoes

Preparation Time: 15 minutes
Cooking Time: 14 minutes
Servings: 2

Ingredients:

- 2 large tomatoes
- ½ cup broccoli, chopped finely
- ½ cup cheddar cheese, shredded
- 1 tablespoon unsalted butter, melted
- ½ teaspoon dried thyme, crushed

Preparation:

1. Carefully cut the top of each tomato and scoop out pulp and seeds.
2. In a bowl, place the chopped broccoli and cheese and mix.
3. Stuff each tomato with broccoli mixture evenly.
4. Arrange the "Crisper Basket" in the pot of Ninja Foodi Grill.
5. Close the Ninja Foodi Grill with lid and select "Air Crisp".
6. Set the temperature to 355 degrees F to preheat.
7. Press "Start/Stop" to begin preheating.
8. When the display shows "Add Food" open the lid and place the tomatoes into the "Crisper Basket".
9. Drizzle the tomatoes with the butter.
10. Close the Ninja Foodi Grill with lid and set the time for 15 minutes.
11. Press "Start/Stop" to begin cooking.
12. When cooking time is completed, press "Start/Stop" to stop cooking and open the lid.
13. Serve with the garnishing of thyme.

Serving Suggestions: Enjoy with fresh baby greens.

Variation Tip: You can use cheese of your choice in this recipe.

Nutritional Information per Serving:

Calories: 206 | **Fat:** 15.6g|**Sat Fat:** 9.7g|**Carbohydrates:** 9.1g|**Fiber:** 2.9g|**Sugar:** 5.3g|**Protein:** 9.4g

Herbed Mushrooms

Preparation Time: 15 minutes
Cooking Time: 8 minutes
Servings: 2

Ingredients:

- 8 ounces button mushrooms, stemmed
- 2 tablespoons olive oil
- 2 tablespoons Italian dried mixed herbs
- Salt and freshly ground black pepper, to taste
- 1 teaspoon dried dill

Preparation:

1. Wash and trim thin slices from the ends of the stems.
2. In a bowl, mix together the mushrooms, dried herbs, oil, salt and black pepper.
3. Arrange the greased "Crisper Basket" in the pot of Ninja Foodi Grill.
4. Close the Ninja Foodi Grill with lid and select "Air Crisp".
5. Set the temperature to 355 degrees F to preheat.
6. Press "Start/Stop" to begin preheating.
7. When the display shows "Add Food" open the lid and place the mushrooms hollow part upwards into the "Crisper Basket".
8. Close the Ninja Foodi Grill with lid and set the time for 8 minutes.
9. Press "Start/Stop" to begin cooking.
10. When cooking time is completed, press "Start/Stop" to stop cooking and open the lid.
11. Serve with the garnishing of dill.

Serving Suggestions: Enjoy these mushrooms with lamb chops.

Variation Tip: Any kind of fresh mushrooms can be used.

Nutritional Information per Serving:

Calories: 149 | **Fat:** 14.4g|**Sat Fat:** 2g|**Carbohydrates:** 4.7g|**Fiber:** 1.7g|**Sugar:** 2g|**Protein:** 3.8g

Glazed Carrots

Preparation Time: 10 minutes
Cooking Time: 12 minutes
Servings: 4

Ingredients:

- 3 cups carrots, peeled and cut into large chunks
- 1 tablespoon olive oil
- 1 tablespoon honey
- 1 tablespoon fresh thyme, finely chopped
- Salt and freshly ground black pepper, to taste

Preparation:

1. In a bowl, add the carrot, oil, honey, thyme, salt and black pepper and mix until well combined.
2. Arrange the "Crisper Basket" in the pot of Ninja Foodi Grill.
3. Close the Ninja Foodi Grill with lid and select "Air Crisp".
4. Set the temperature to 390 degrees F to preheat.
5. Press "Start/Stop" to begin preheating.
6. When the display shows "Add Food" open the lid and place the carrot chunks into the "Crisper Basket" in a single layer.
7. Close the Ninja Foodi Grill with lid and set the time for 12 minutes.
8. Press "Start/Stop" to begin cooking.
9. When the cooking time is completed, press "Start/Stop" to stop cooking and open the lid.
10. Serve hot.

Serving Suggestions: Serve with the garnishing ogf fresh dill.

Variation Tip: Honey can be replaced with maple syrup.

Nutritional Information per Serving:

Calories: 82 | **Fat:** 3.6g|**Sat Fat:** 0.5g|**Carbohydrates:** 12.9g|**Fiber:** 0.3g|**Sugar:** 8.4g|**Protein:** 0.8g

Lemony Green Beans

Preparation Time: 10 minutes
Cooking Time: 12 minutes
Servings: 4

Ingredients:

- 1 pound fresh green beans, trimmed
- 1 tablespoon butter, melted
- 1 tablespoon fresh lemon juice
- ¼ teaspoon garlic powder
- Salt and freshly ground black pepper, to taste
- ½ teaspoon lemon zest, grated

Preparation:

1. In a large bowl, add all the ingredients except the lemon zest and toss to coat well.
2. Arrange the "Crisper Basket" in the pot of Ninja Foodi Grill.
3. Close the Ninja Foodi Grill with lid and select "Air Crisp".
4. Set the temperature to 400 degrees F to preheat.
5. Press "Start/Stop" to begin preheating.
6. When the display shows "Add Food" open the lid and place the green beans into the "Crisper Basket".
7. Close the Ninja Foodi Grill with lid and set the time for 12 minutes.
8. Press "Start/Stop" to begin cooking.
9. When the cooking time is completed, press "Start/Stop" to stop cooking and open the lid.
10. Serve warm with the garnishing of lemon zest.

Serving Suggestions: Serve with the topping of feta cheese.

Variation Tip: Use freshly squeezed lemon juice.

Nutritional Information per Serving:

Calories: 62 | **Fat:** 3.1g | **Sat Fat:** 1.9g | **Carbohydrates:** 8.4g | **Fiber:** 3.9g | **Sugar:** 1.7g | **Protein:** 2.2g

Vinegar Brussels Sprout

Preparation Time: 10 minutes
Cooking Time: 20 minutes
Servings: 4

Ingredients:

- 1 pound Brussels sprouts, ends trimmed and cut into bite-sized pieces
- 1 tablespoon balsamic vinegar
- 1 tablespoon olive oil
- Salt and freshly ground black pepper, to taste

Preparation:

1. In a bowl, add all the ingredients and toss to coat well.
2. Arrange the "Crisper Basket" in the pot of Ninja Foodi Grill.
3. Close the Ninja Foodi Grill with lid and select "Air Crisp".
4. Set the temperature to 350 degrees F to preheat.
5. Press "Start/Stop" to begin preheating.
6. When the display shows "Add Food" open the lid and place the Brussels sprouts into the "Crisper Basket".
7. Close the Ninja Foodi Grill with lid and set the time for 20 minutes.
8. Press "Start/Stop" to begin cooking.
9. When the cooking time is completed, press "Start/Stop" to stop cooking and open the lid.
10. Serve hot.

Serving Suggestions: Serve with the topping of pine nuts.

Variation Tip: Red wine vinegar will also work nicely in this recipe.

Nutritional Information per Serving:

Calories: 80 | **Fat:** 3.9g|**Sat Fat:** 0.6g|**Carbohydrates:** 10.3g|**Fiber:** 4.3g|**Sugar:** 2.5g|**Protein:** 3.9g

Nutty Acorn Squash

Preparation Time: 10 minutes
Cooking Time: 25 minutes
Servings: 2

Ingredients:

- 1 medium acorn squash
- 2 teaspoons olive oil
- 2 tablespoons pecans, chopped
- 1 tablespoon brown sugar
- ½ teaspoon ground cinnamon
- 1/8 teaspoon ground cloves

Preparation:

1. Cut the acorn squash in half lengthwise.
2. Brush the flesh side of each squash half with oil.
3. In a bowl, add the remaining ingredients and mix.
4. Arrange the "Crisper Basket" in the pot of Ninja Foodi Grill.
5. Close the Ninja Foodi Grill with lid and select "Air Crisp".
6. Set the temperature to 375 degrees F to preheat.
7. Press "Start/Stop" to begin preheating.
8. When the display shows "Add Food" open the lid and place the squash halves, cut side up into the "Crisper Basket".
9. Close the Ninja Foodi Grill with lid and set the time for 25 minutes.
10. Press "Start/Stop" to begin cooking.
11. When the cooking time is completed, press "Start/Stop" to stop cooking and open the lid.
12. Serve warm.

Serving Suggestions: Serve with the sprinkling of extra cinnamon.

Variation Tip: Butter can be used instead of oil.

Nutritional Information per Serving:

Calories: 254 | **Fat:** 11.1g | **Sat Fat:** 1.4g | **Carbohydrates:** 41.6g | **Fiber:** 6.4g | **Sugar:** 4.7g | **Protein:** 3.7g

Stuffed Potatoes

Preparation Time: 15 minutes
Cooking Time: 26 minutes
Servings: 4

Ingredients:

- 4 potatoes, peeled
- 2-3 tablespoons canola oil
- 1 tablespoon butter
- ½ of brown onion, chopped
- 2 tablespoons fresh chives, chopped
- ½ cup Parmesan cheese, grated

Preparation:

1. Coat the potatoes with some oil.
2. Arrange the "Crisper Basket" in the pot of Ninja Foodi Grill.
3. Close the Ninja Foodi Grill with lid and select "Air Crisp".
4. Set the temperature to 390 degrees F to preheat.
5. Press "Start/Stop" to begin preheating.
6. When the display shows "Add Food" open the lid and place the potatoes into the "Crisper Basket".
7. Close the Ninja Foodi Grill with lid and set the time for 20 minutes.
8. Press "Start/Stop" to begin cooking.
9. Coat the potatoes twice with the remaining oil.
10. Meanwhile, in a frying pan, melt the butter over medium heat and sauté the onion for about 4-5 minutes.
11. Remove from the heat and transfer the onion into a bowl.
12. In the bowl of onion, add the potato flesh, chives, and half of cheese and stir to combine.
13. When cooking time is completed, press "Start/Stop" to stop cooking and open the lid.
14. Transfer the potatoes onto a platter.
15. Carefully cut each potato in half.
16. With a small scooper, scoop out the flesh from each half.
17. Stuff the potato halves with potato mixture evenly and sprinkle with the remaining cheese.
18. Again, arrange the potato halves in the "Crisper Basket".
19. Close the Ninja Foodi Grill with lid and select "Air Crisp".
20. Set the temperature to 390 degrees F for 6 minutes.
21. Press "Start/Stop" to begin cooking.

22. When cooking time is completed, press "Start/Stop" to stop cooking and open the lid.
23. Serve immediately.

Serving Suggestions: Serve with fresh lettuce.

Variation Tip: You can use herbs of your choice.

Nutritional Information per Serving:

Calories: 276 | **Fat:** 12.5g|**Sat Fat:** 3.6g|**Carbohydrates:** 34.8g|**Fiber:** 5.4g|**Sugar:** 3.1g|**Protein:** 7.8g

Vegetarian Stuffed Bell Peppers

Preparation Time: 15 minutes
Cooking Time: 15 minutes
Servings: 5

Ingredients:

- ½ of small bell pepper, seeded and chopped
- 1 (15-ounce) can diced tomatoes with juice
- 1 (15-ounce) can red kidney beans, rinsed and drained
- 1 cup cooked rice
- 1½ teaspoons Italian seasoning
- 5 large bell peppers, tops removed and seeded
- ½ cup mozzarella cheese, shredded
- 1 tablespoon Parmesan cheese, grated

Preparation:

1. In a bowl, mix together the chopped bell pepper, tomatoes with juice, beans, rice, and Italian seasoning.
2. Stuff each bell pepper with the rice mixture.
3. Arrange the greased "Crisper Basket" in the pot of Ninja Foodi Grill.
4. Close the Ninja Foodi Grill with lid and select "Air Crisp".
5. Set the temperature to 360 degrees F to preheat.
6. Press "Start/Stop" to begin preheating.
7. When the display shows "Add Food" open the lid and place the bell peppers into the "Crisper Basket".
8. Close the Ninja Foodi Grill with lid and set the time for 15 minutes.
9. Press "Start/Stop" to begin cooking.
10. Meanwhile, in a bowl, mix together the mozzarella and Parmesan cheese.
11. After 12 minutes of cooking, top each bell pepper with cheese mixture.
12. When cooking time is completed, press "Start/Stop" to stop cooking and open the lid.
13. Transfer the bell peppers onto a serving platter and serve warm.

Serving Suggestions: You

Variation Tip: Don't forget to remove the seeds from bell peppers.

Nutritional Information per Serving:

Calories: 282 | **Fat:** 2.8g|**Sat Fat:** 1.1g|**Carbohydrates:** 54.9g|**Fiber:** 9.2g|
Sugar: 8.3g|**Protein:** 11.4g

Green Beans Casserole

Preparation Time: 15 minutes
Cooking Time: 32 minutes
Servings: 6

Ingredients:

- 1½ pounds fresh green beans, trimmed
- 2 cups fresh mushrooms, chopped
- 1 cup onion, chopped
- 1 tablespoon all-purpose flour
- 1 (14-ounce) can full-fat coconut milk
- ¾ cup vegetable broth

Preparation:

1. In a pan of boiling water, add the green beans and cook for about 5-7 minutes.
2. Drain the green beans and rinse in cold water.
3. Drain again and set aside.
4. In a skillet, heat the oil over medium heat and sauté the mushrooms and onions for about 5-6 minutes.
5. Add the flour and stir to combine.
6. Stir in the coconut milk and broth and remove from the heat.
7. In the bottom of a greased baking pan, place the cooked green beans and top with broth mixture.
8. Arrange the "Crisper Basket" in the pot of Ninja Foodi Grill.
9. Close the Ninja Foodi Grill with lid and select "Air Crisp".
10. Set the temperature to 370 degrees F to preheat.
11. Press "Start/Stop" to begin preheating.
12. When the display shows "Add Food" open the lid and place the pan into the "Crisper Basket".
13. Close the Ninja Foodi Grill with lid and set the time for 15 minutes.
14. Press "Start/Stop" to begin cooking.
15. When cooking time is completed, press "Start/Stop" to stop cooking and open the lid.
16. Serve warm.

Serving Suggestions: You can top this casserole with fried onions.

Variation Tip: You can add seasoning of yor choice in this recipe.

Nutritional Information per Serving:

Calories: 179 | **Fat:** 12.6g | **Sat Fat:** 11.3g | **Carbohydrates:** 13.8g | **Fiber:** 4.5g | **Sugar:** 3.9g | **Protein:** 4.8g

Tofu with Orange Sauce

Preparation Time: 15 minutes
Cooking Time: 20 minutes
Servings: 4

Ingredients:

For Tofu:

- 1 pound extra-firm tofu, pressed and cubed
- 1 tablespoon cornstarch
- 1 tablespoon tamari

For Sauce

- ½ cup water
- 1/3 cup fresh orange juice
- 1 tablespoon honey
- 1 teaspoon orange zest, grated
- 1 teaspoon garlic, minced
- 1 teaspoon fresh ginger, minced
- 2 teaspoons cornstarch
- ¼ teaspoon red pepper flakes, crushed

Preparation:

1. In a bowl, add the tofu, cornstarch, and tamari and toss to coat well.
2. Set the tofu aside to marinate for at least 15 minutes.
3. Arrange the greased "Crisper Basket" in the pot of Ninja Foodi Grill.
4. Close the Ninja Ninja Foodi Grill with lid and select "Air Crisp".
5. Set the temperature to 390 degrees F to preheat.
6. Press "Start/Stop" to begin preheating.
7. When the display shows "Add Food" open the lid and place the tofu cubes into the "Crisper Ninja Foodi Grill with lid and set the time for 10 minutes.
8. Press "Start/Stop" to begin cooking.
9. Meanwhile, for the sauce: in a small pan, add all the ingredients over medium-high heat and bring to a boil, stirring continuously.
10. When the cooking time is completed, press "Start/Stop" to stop cooking.
11. Open the lid and transfer the tofu into a serving bowl.
12. Add the sauce and gently stir to combine.
13. Serve immediately.

Serving Suggestions: Enjoy with the garnishing of scallion greens.

Variation Tip: Make sure to use freshly squeezed orage juice.

Nutritional Information per Serving:

Calories: 147 | **Fat:** 6.7g|**Sat Fat:** 0.6g|**Carbohydrates:** 12.7g|**Fiber:** 0.7g| **Sugar:** 6.7g|**Protein:** 12.1g

Beef, Pork & Lamb Recipes

Herbed Beef Roast

Preparation Time: 10 minutes
Cooking Time: 45 minutes
Servings: 5

Ingredients:

- 2 pounds beef roast
- 1 tablespoon olive oil
- 1 teaspoon dried rosemary, crushed
- 1 teaspoon dried thyme, crushed
- Salt, to taste

Preparation:

1. In a bowl, mix together the oil, herbs, and salt.
2. Rub the roast with herb mixture generously.
3. Arrange the greased "Crisper Basket" in the pot of Ninja Foodi Grill.
4. Close the Ninja Foodi Grill with lid and select "Air Crisp".
5. Set the temperature to 360 degrees F to preheat.
6. Press "Start/Stop" to begin preheating.
7. When the display shows "Add Food" open the lid and place the roast into the "Crisper Basket".
8. Close the Ninja Foodi Grill with lid and set the time for 45 minutes.
9. Press "Start/Stop" to begin cooking.
10. When cooking time is completed, press "Start/Stop" to stop cooking and open the lid.
11. Place the roast onto a platter.
12. With a piece of foil, cover the roast for about 10 minutes before slicing.
13. Cut the roast into desired size slices and serve.

Serving Suggestions: Glazed carrots will be great if served with roast.

Variation Tip: Good, fresh meat should be firm, not tough or soft.

Nutritional Information per Serving:

Calories: 2001 | **Fat:** 8.8g|**Sat Fat:** 3.1g|**Carbohydrates:** 0g|**Fiber:** 0g|**Sugar:** 0g|**Protein:** 28.9g

Bacon-Wrapped Beef Tenderloin

Preparation Time: 10 minutes
Cooking Time: 12 minutes
Servings: 4

Ingredients:

- 8 bacon strips
- 4 (8-ounce) center-cut beef tenderloin filets
- 2 tablespoons olive oil, divided
- Salt and freshly ground black pepper, to taste

Preparation:

1. Wrap 2 bacon strips around the entire outside of each beef filet.
2. With toothpicks, secure each filet.
3. Coat each wrapped filet with oil and sprinkle with salt and black pepper evenly.
4. Arrange the "Grill Grate" in the pot of Ninja Foodi Grill.
5. Close the Ninja Foodi Grill with lid and select "Grill" to "High" to preheat.
6. Press "Start/Stop" to begin preheating.
7. When the display shows "Add Food" open the lid and place the wrapped filets onto the "Grill Grate".
8. With your hands, gently press down each filet.
9. Close the Ninja Foodi Grill with lid and set the time for 12 minutes.
10. Press "Start/Stop" to begin cooking.
11. After 6 minutes of cooking, flip the filets.
12. When cooking time is completed, press "Start/Stop" to stop cooking and open the lid.
13. Transfer the filets onto a platter for about 10 minutes before serving.

Serving Suggestions: Serve with romaine lettuce.

Variation Tip: Make sure that tenderloin is bright and pinkish-red in color.

Nutritional Information per Serving:

Calories: 841 | **Fat:** 52g|**Sat Fat:** 16.9g|**Carbohydrates:** 0.8g|**Fiber:** 0g|**Sugar:** 0.1g|**Protein:** 87.1g

Seasoned Rib-Eye Steak

Preparation Time: 10 minutes
Cooking Time: 12 minutes
Servings: 8

Ingredients:

- 2 (1½-pound) rib-eye steaks
- 3-4 tablespoons steak seasoning
- Salt and freshly ground black pepper, to taste

Preparation:

1. Season steaks with steak seasoning, salt and black pepper.
2. Set aside at room temperature for about 30 minutes.
3. Arrange the "Grill Grate" in the pot of Ninja Foodi Grill.
4. Close the Ninja Foodi Grill with lid and select "Grill" to "High" to preheat.
5. Press "Start/Stop" to begin preheating.
6. When the display shows "Add Food" open the lid and place the steaks onto the "Grill Grate".
7. With your hands, gently press down each steak.
8. Close the Ninja Foodi Grill with lid and set the time for 12 minutes.
9. Press "Start/Stop" to begin cooking.
10. After 6 minutes of cooking, flip the steaks.
11. When cooking time is completed, press "Start/Stop" to stop cooking and open the lid.
12. Place the steaks onto a cutting board for about 5 minutes before slicing.
13. Cut into desired sized slices and stir with the pot sauce.
14. Serve hot.

Serving Suggestions: Enjoy with savory quinoa.

Variation Tip: You can use seasoning if your choice.

Nutritional Information per Serving:

Calories: 467 | **Fat:** 37.6g | **Sat Fat:** 15.1g | **Carbohydrates:** 0g | **Fiber:** 0g | **Sugar:** 0g | **Protein:** 30.1g

Beef Casserole

Preparation Time: 10 minutes
Cooking Time: 25 minutes
Servings: 6

Ingredients:

- 2 pounds ground beef
- 2 tablespoons taco seasoning
- 1 cup cheddar cheese, shredded
- 1 cup cottage cheese
- 1 cup salsa

Preparation:

1. In a bowl, add the beef and taco seasoning and mix well.
2. Add the cheeses and salsa and stir to combine.
3. Place the mixture into a greased baking pan.
4. With a spoon, press the mixture slightly to smooth the top surface.
5. Arrange the "Crisper Basket" in the pot of Ninja Foodi Grill.
6. Close the Ninja Foodi Grill with lid and select "Bake".
7. Set the temperature to 370 degrees F to preheat.
8. Press "Start/Stop" to begin preheating.
9. When the display shows "Add Food" open the lid and place the pan into the "Crisper Basket".
10. Close the Ninja Foodi Grill with lid and set the time for 25 minutes.
11. Press "Start/Stop" to begin cooking.
12. When cooking time is completed, press "Start/Stop" to stop cooking and open the lid.
13. Serve warm.

Serving Suggestions: Enjoy with lemony Brussel Sprouts.

Variation Tip: Don't forget to grease the baking pan.

Nutritional Information per Serving:

Calories: 412 | **Fat:** 16.5g | **Sat Fat:** 8g | **Carbohydrates:** 6.3g | **Fiber:** 0.7g | **Sugar:** 2.1g | **Protein:** 56.4g

Beef Stuffed Bell Peppers

Preparation Time: 15 minutes
Cooking Time: 25 minutes
Servings: 6

Ingredients:

- 6 green bell peppers
- 1¼ pounds lean ground beef
- 1 cup marinara sauce
- 1/3 cup scallion, chopped
- ¼ cup fresh parsley, chopped
- ½ teaspoon dried sage, crushed
- ½ teaspoon garlic salt
- 1 tablespoon olive oil
- ¼ cup mozzarella cheese, shredded

Preparation:

1. Cut the top off of each bell pepper and Carefully remove the seeds. Set aside.
2. Heat a nonstick skillet over medium-high heat and cook the beef for about 8-10 minutes.
3. Drain the grease completely.
4. Add the marinara sauce, scallion, parsley, sage, salt and oil and mix well.
5. Stuff each bell pepper with beef mixture.
6. Arrange the greased "Crisper Basket" in the pot of Ninja Foodi Grill.
7. Close the Ninja Foodi Grill with lid and select "Air Crisp".
8. Set the temperature to 355 degrees F to preheat.
9. Press "Start/Stop" to begin preheating.
10. When the display shows "Add Food" open the lid and place the bell peppers into the "Crisper Basket".
11. Close the Ninja Foodi Grill with lid and set the time for 25 minutes.
12. Press "Start/Stop" to begin cooking.
13. After 10 minutes of cooking, top each bell pepper with cheese.
14. When cooking time is completed, press "Start/Stop" to stop cooking and open the lid.
15. Serve hot.

Serving Suggestions: Serve with the drizzling of lemon juice.

Variation Tip: You can replace ground turkey with beef.

Nutritional Information per Serving:

Calories: 263 | **Fat:** 9.8g|**Sat Fat:** 3.3g|**Carbohydrates:** 12.1g|**Fiber:** 3.4g|**Sugar:** 6.8g|**Protein:** 31g

Glazed Pork Ribs

Preparation Time: 10 minutes
Cooking Time: 13 minutes
Servings: 6

Ingredients:

- ¾ cup tomato sauce
- 3 tablespoons honey
- 1 tablespoon Worcestershire sauce
- 1 tablespoon low-sodium soy sauce
- 1 tablespoon fresh lime juice
- ½ teaspoon garlic powder
- ½ teaspoon red pepper flakes, crushed
- Freshly ground black pepper, to taste
- 2 pounds pork ribs

Preparation:

1. In a large bowl, add all the ingredients except pork ribs and mix well.
2. Add the pork ribs ad coat with the mixture generously.
3. Arrange the greased "Crisper Basket" in the pot of Ninja Foodi Grill.
4. Close the Ninja Foodi Grill with lid and select "Air Crisp".
5. Set the temperature to 355 degrees F to preheat.
6. Press "Start/Stop" to begin preheating.
7. When the display shows "Add Food" open the lid and place the pork ribs into the "Crisper Basket".
8. Close the Ninja Foodi Grill with lid and set the time for 13 minutes.
9. Press "Start/Stop" to begin cooking.
10. Flip the ribs once halfway through.
11. When cooking time is completed, press "Start/Stop" to stop cooking and open the lid.
12. Transfer the ribs onto a platter for about 5 minutes before serving.

Serving Suggestions: Serve with sour cream and cheddar mashed potatoes.

Variation Tip: Look for ribs that are pinkish-red in color.

Nutritional Information per Serving:

Calories: 457 | **Fat:** 26.9g|**Sat Fat:** 9.5g|**Carbohydrates:** 11.3g|**Fiber:** 0.6g|**Sugar:** 10.7g|**Protein:** 40.7g

Pork Loin with Potatoes

Preparation Time: 10 minutes
Cooking Time: 25 minutes
Servings: 6

Ingredients:

- 2 pounds pork loin
- 3 tablespoons olive oil, divided
- 1 teaspoon fresh parsley, chopped
- Salt and freshly ground black pepper, to taste
- 3 large red potatoes, chopped
- ½ teaspoon garlic powder
- ½ teaspoon red pepper flakes, crushed

Preparation:

1. Coat the pork loin with oil and then, season evenly with parsley, salt, and black pepper.
2. In a large bowl, add the potatoes, remaining oil, garlic powder, red pepper flakes, salt, and black pepper and toss to coat well.
3. Arrange the greased "Crisper Basket" in the pot of Ninja Foodi Grill.
4. Close the Ninja Foodi Grill with lid and select "Air Crisp".
5. Set the temperature to 325 degrees F to preheat.
6. Press "Start/Stop" to begin preheating.
7. When the display shows "Add Food" open the lid and place the pork loin into the "Crisper Basket".
8. Arrange the potato pieces around the pork loin.
9. Close the Ninja Foodi Grill with lid and set the time for 25 minutes.
10. Press "Start/Stop" to begin cooking.
11. When cooking time is completed, press "Start/Stop" to stop cooking and open the lid.
12. Place the pork loin onto a platter for about 5 minutes before slicing.
13. Cut the pork loin into desired size slices and serve alongside the potatoes.

Serving Suggestions: Serve with a topping of herbed butter.

Variation Tip: Place the pork loin, fat side up in the basket.

Nutritional Information per Serving:

Calories: 555 | **Fat:** 28.3g|**Sat Fat:** 9g|**Carbohydrates:** 29.2g|**Fiber:** 4.5g|
Sugar: 2.2g|**Protein:** 44.5g

Garlicky Pork Tenderloin

Preparation Time: 10 minutes
Cooking Time: 20 minutes
Servings: 5

Ingredients:

- 1½ pounds pork tenderloin
- Nonstick cooking spray
- 2 small heads roasted garlic
- Salt and ground black pepper, as required

Preparation:

1. Lightly spray all sides of pork with cooking spray and then season with salt and black pepper.
2. Now, rub the pork with roasted garlic.
3. Arrange the roast onto the lightly greased baking pan.
4. Arrange the "Crisper Basket" in the pot of Ninja Foodi Grill.
5. Close the Ninja Foodi Grill with lid and select "Air Crisp".
6. Set the temperature to 400 degrees F to preheat.
7. Press "Start/Stop" to begin preheating.
8. When the display shows "Add Food" open the lid and place the pan into the "Crisper Basket".
9. Close the Ninja Foodi Grill with lid and set the time for 20 minutes.
10. Press "Start/Stop" to begin cooking.
11. Flip the pork tenderloin once halfway through.
12. When cooking time is completed, press "Start/Stop" to stop cooking and open the lid.
13. Place the pork tenderloin onto a platter for about 10 minutes before slicing.
14. With a sharp knife, cut the pork tenderloin into desired sized slices and serve.

Serving Suggestions: Serve with charred snap peas.

Variation Tip: Season the pork tenderloin evenly.

Nutritional Information per Serving:

Calories: 202 | **Fat:** 4.8g | **Sat Fat:** 1.6g | **Carbohydrates:** 1.7g | **Fiber:** 0.1g | **Sugar:** 0.1g | **Protein:** 35.9g

Glazed Ham

Preparation Time: 15 minutes
Cooking Time: 40 minutes
Servings: 4

Ingredients:

- 1 pound 10½ ounces ham
- 1 cup whiskey
- 2 tablespoons French mustard
- 2 tablespoons honey

Preparation:

1. Place the ham at room temperature for about 30 minutes before cooking.
2. In a bowl, mix together the whiskey, mustard and honey.
3. Place the ham in a baking pan.
4. Top with half of the honey mixture and coat well.
5. Arrange the "Crisper Basket" in the pot of Ninja Foodi Grill.
6. Close the Ninja Foodi Grill with lid and select "Air Crisp".
7. Set the temperature to 320 degrees F to preheat.
8. Press "Start/Stop" to begin preheating.
9. When the display shows "Add Food" open the lid and place the pan into the "Crisper Basket".
10. Close the Ninja Foodi Grill with lid and set the time for 40 minutes.
11. Press "Start/Stop" to begin cooking.
12. After 15 minutes of cooking, flip the side of ham and top with the remaining honey mixture.
13. When cooking time is completed, press "Start/Stop" to stop cooking and open the lid.
14. Place the ham onto a platter for about 10 minutes before slicing.
15. Cut the ham into desired size slices and serve.

Serving Suggestions: Serve with crispy smashed potatoes with caper gremolata.

Variation Tip: The sweetness should be balanced with whiskey.

Nutritional Information per Serving:

Calories: 477 | **Fat:** 16.2g|**Sat Fat:** 5.5g|**Carbohydrates:** 15.9g|**Fiber:** 2.5g|**Sugar:** 8.7g|**Protein:** 31.2g

Pork & Sausage Meatloaf

Preparation Time: 15 minutes
Cooking Time: 25 minutes
Servings: 4

Ingredients:

- 14 ounces lean ground pork
- 1 gluten-free chorizo sausage, chopped finely
- 1 small onion, chopped
- 1 garlic clove, minced
- 2 tablespoons fresh cilantro, chopped
- 3 tablespoons breadcrumbs
- 1 egg
- Salt and freshly ground black pepper, to taste
- 2 tablespoons fresh mushrooms, sliced thinly
- 2 tablespoons olive oil

Preparation:

1. In a large bowl, add all ingredients except mushrooms and mix until well combined.
2. In a baking pan, place the beef mixture and with the back of a spatula, smooth the surface.
3. Top with mushroom slices and gently, press into the meatloaf.
4. Drizzle with oil evenly.
5. Arrange the "Crisper Basket" in the pot of Ninja Foodi Grill.
6. Close the Ninja Foodi Grill with lid and select "Air Crisp".
7. Set the temperature to 390 degrees F to preheat.
8. Press "Start/Stop" to begin preheating.
9. When the display shows "Add Food" open the lid and place the pan into the "Crisper Basket".
10. Close the Ninja Foodi Grill with lid and set the time for 25 minutes.
11. Press "Start/Stop" to begin cooking.
12. When cooking time is completed, press "Start/Stop" to stop cooking and open the lid.
13. Cut the meatloaf into desired sized slices and serve.

Serving Suggestions: Roasted broccoli will go great with this meatloaf.

Variation Tip: Make sure to use fresh mushrooms.

Nutritional Information per Serving:

Calories: 361 | **Fat:** 28.1g|**Sat Fat:** 3g|**Carbohydrates:** 5.6g|**Fiber:** 0.7g|**Sugar:** 1.1g|**Protein:** 22g

Glazed Leg of Lamb

Preparation Time: 15 minutes
Cooking Time: 1 hour 40 minutes
Servings: 10

Ingredients:

- ¼ cup olive oil
- 4 garlic cloves, chopped
- ¼ cup fresh rosemary
- 3 tablespoons Dijon mustard
- 2 tablespoons maple syrup
- Salt and freshly ground black pepper, to taste
- 1 (4-pound) leg of lamb

Preparation:

1. In a food processor, add the oil, garlic, herbs, mustard, honey, salt and black pepper and pulse until smooth.
2. Place the leg of lamb and marinade into a glass baking dish and mix well
3. With plastic wrap, cover the baking dish and refrigerate to marinate for 6-8 hours.
4. Arrange a wire rack in a baking pan.
5. Arrange the leg of lamb into the prepared baking pan.
6. Arrange the "Crisper Basket" in the pot of Ninja Foodi Grill.
7. Close the Ninja Foodi Grill with lid and select "Bake".
8. Set the temperature to42 degrees F to preheat.
9. Press "Start/Stop" to begin preheating.
10. When the display shows "Add Food" open the lid and place the pan into the "Crisper Basket".
11. Close the Ninja Foodi Grill with lid and set the time for 1 hour and 20 minutes.
12. Press "Start/Stop" to begin cooking.
13. When cooking time is completed, press "Start/Stop" to stop cooking and open the lid.
14. Place the leg of lamb onto a cutting board.
15. With a piece of foil, cover the leg of lamb for about 10 minutes before slicing.
16. With a sharp knife, cut the leg of lamb into desired size slices and serve.

Serving Suggestions: Mashed potatoes make a classic pairing with leg of lamb.

Variation Tip: Avoid to buy leg of lamb with darker meat and yellow fat.

Nutritional Information per Serving:

Calories: 401 | **Fat:** 18.8g|**Sat Fat:** 5.6g|**Carbohydrates:** 4.3g|**Fiber:** 0.8g|
Sugar: 2.4g|**Protein:** 51.3g

Pesto Rack of Lamb

Preparation Time: 15 minutes
Cooking Time: 15 minutes
Servings: 4

Ingredients:

- ½ bunch fresh mint
- 1 garlic clove
- ¼ cup extra-virgin olive oil
- ½ tablespoons honey
- Salt and freshly ground black pepper, to taste
- 1 (1½-pound) rack of lamb

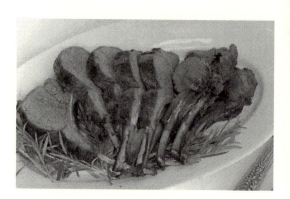

Preparation:

1. For pesto: in a blender, add the mint, garlic, oil, honey, salt, and black pepper and pulse until smooth.
2. Coat the rack of lamb with some pesto evenly.
3. Arrange the greased "Crisper Basket" in the pot of Ninja Foodi Grill.
4. Close the Ninja Foodi Grill with lid and select "Air Crisp".
5. Set the temperature to 200 degrees F to preheat.
6. Press "Start/Stop" to begin preheating.
7. When the display shows "Add Food" open the lid and place the rack of lamb into the "Crisper Basket".
8. Close the Ninja Foodi Grill with lid and set the time for 15 minutes.
9. Press "Start/Stop" to begin cooking.
10. While cooking, coat the rack of lamb with the remaining pesto after every 5 minutes.
11. When the cooking time is completed, press "Start/Stop" to stop cooking and open the lid.
12. Open the lid and place the rack of lamb onto a cutting board for about 5 minutes.
13. Cut the rack into individual chops and serve.

Serving Suggestions: Serve with the drizzling of lemon juice.

Variation Tip: Make sure to remove the silver skin from the rack of lamb.

Nutritional Information per Serving:

Calories: 405 | **Fat:** 27.7g|**Sat Fat:** 7.1g|**Carbohydrates:** 2.8g|**Fiber:** 0.3g|**Sugar:** 2.2g|**Protein:** 34.8g

Garlicky Lamb Chops

Preparation Time: 10 minutes
Cooking Time: 15 minutes
Servings: 4

Ingredients:

- 4 garlic cloves, crushed
- 1 tablespoon fresh lemon juice
- 1 teaspoon olive oil
- 1 tablespoon Za'atar
- Kosher salt and ground black pepper, as required
- 8 (3½-ounces) bone-in lamb loin chops, trimmed

Preparation:

1. In a large bowl, mix together the garlic, lemon juice, oil, Za'atar, salt and black pepper.
2. Coat the chops with the garlic mixture.
3. Arrange the greased "Crisper Basket" in the pot of Ninja Foodi Grill.
4. Close the Ninja Foodi Grill with lid and select "Air Crisp".
5. Set the temperature to 400 degrees F to preheat.
6. Press "Start/Stop" to begin preheating.
7. When the display shows "Add Food" open the lid and place the chops into the "Crisper Basket".
8. Close the Ninja Foodi Grill with lid and set the time for 15 minutes.
9. Press "Start/Stop" to begin cooking.
10. Flip the chops once halfway through.
11. When the cooking time is completed, press "Start/Stop" to stop cooking and open the lid and
12. Serve hot.

Serving Suggestions: Serve with the oasted potatoes.

Variation Tip: Lemon juice can be replaced with vinegar.

Nutritional Information per Serving:

Calories: 385 | **Fat:** 15.8g|**Sat Fat:** 5.4g|**Carbohydrates:** 1.1g|**Fiber:** 0.1g|**Sugar:** 0.1g|**Protein:** 55.9g

Sweet & Sour Lamb Chops

Preparation Time: 10 minutes
Cooking Time: 40 minutes
Servings: 3

Ingredients:

- 3 (8-ounce) lamb shoulder chops
- Salt and freshly ground black pepper, to taste
- ¼ cup sugar
- 2 tablespoons fresh lime juice

Preparation:

1. Season the lamb chops with salt and black pepper generously.in a baking pan, place the chops and sprinkle with sugar, followed by the lime juice.
2. Arrange the "Crisper Basket" in the pot of Ninja Foodi Grill.
3. Close the Ninja Foodi Grill with lid and select "Roast".
4. Set the temperature to 376 degrees F to preheat.
5. Press "Start/Stop" to begin preheating.
6. When the display shows "Add Food" open the lid and place the chops into the "Crisper Basket".
7. Close the Ninja Foodi Grill with lid and set the time for 40 minutes.
8. Press "Start/Stop" to begin cooking.
9. After 20 minutes of cooking, flip the chops and coat with the pan juices.
10. When cooking time is completed, press "Start/Stop" to stop cooking and open the lid.
11. Serve hot.

Serving Suggestions: Serve with fresh greens.

Variation Tip: sugar can be replaced with honey.

Nutritional Information per Serving:

Calories: 405 | **Fat:** 18.1g|**Sat Fat:** 6g|**Carbohydrates:** 16.8g|**Fiber:** 0g|**Sugar:** 16.7g|**Protein:** 44.2g

Dessert Recipes

Stuffed Apples

Preparation Time: 10 minutes
Cooking Time: 10 minutes
Servings: 4

Ingredients:

For Stuffed Apples:

- 4 small firm apples, cored
- ½ cup golden raisins
- ½ cup blanched almonds
- 2 tablespoons sugar

For Vanilla Sauce:

- ½ cup whipped cream
- 2 tablespoons sugar
- ½ teaspoon vanilla extract

Preparation:

1. In a food processor, add the raisins, almonds, and sugar and pulse until chopped.
2. Carefully stuff each apple with raisin mixture.
3. Line a baking pan with parchment paper.
4. Place apples into the prepared baking pan.
5. Arrange the "Crisper Basket" in the pot of Ninja Foodi Grill.
6. Close the Ninja Foodi Grill with lid and select "Air Crisp".
7. Set the temperature to 355 degrees F to preheat.
8. Press "Start/Stop" to begin preheating.
9. When the display shows "Add Food" open the lid and place the pan into the "Crisper Basket".
10. Close the Ninja Foodi Grill with lid and set the time for 10 minutes.
11. Press "Start/Stop" to begin cooking.
12. Meanwhile, for vanilla sauce: in a pan, add the cream, sugar, and vanilla extract over medium heat and cook for about 2-3 minutes or until sugar is dissolved, stirring continuously.
13. When the cooking time is completed, press "Start/Stop" to stop cooking and open the lid.
14. Transfer the apples onto the serving plates and set aside to cool slightly
15. Top with the vanilla sauce and serve.

Serving Suggestions: Serve with a sprinkling of nuts.

Variation Tip: Warm vanilla sauce will be great for serving.

Nutritional Information per Serving:

Calories: 329 | **Fat:** 11.1g|**Sat Fat:** 3.4g|**Carbohydrates:** 60.2g|**Fiber:** 7.6g|**Sugar:** 46.5g|**Protein:** 4g

Cranberry Cupcakes

Preparation Time: 15 minutes
Cooking Time: 15 minutes
Servings: 8

Ingredients:

- ¼ cup unsweetened almond milk
- 2 large eggs
- ½ teaspoon vanilla extract
- 1½ cups almond flour
- ¼ cup sugar
- 1 teaspoon baking powder
- ¼ teaspoon ground cinnamon
- 1/8 teaspoon salt

- ½ cup fresh cranberries
- ¼ cup walnuts, chopped

Preparation:

1. In a blender, add the almond milk, eggs and vanilla extract and pulse for about 20-30 seconds.
2. Add the almond flour, sugar, baking powder, cinnamon and salt and pulse for about 30-45 seconds or until well blended.
3. Transfer the mixture into a bowl.
4. Gently fold in half of the cranberries and walnuts.
5. Place the mixture into 8 silicone muffin cups and top each with remaining cranberries.
6. Arrange the "Crisper Basket" in the pot of Ninja Foodi Grill.
7. Close the Ninja Foodi Grill with lid and select "Air Crisp".
8. Set the temperature to 325 degrees F to preheat.
9. Press "Start/Stop" to begin preheating.
10. When the display shows "Add Food" open the lid and place the muffin cups into the "Crisper Basket".
11. Close the Ninja Foodi Grill with lid and set the time for 15 minutes.
12. Press "Start/Stop" to begin cooking.
13. When cooking time is completed, press "Start/Stop" to stop cooking and open the lid.
14. Place the muffin cups onto a wire rack to cool for about 10 minutes.
15. Now, invert the muffins onto the wire rack to cool completely before serving.

Serving Suggestions: Serve with the garnishing of orange zest.

Variation Tip: Fresh cranberries can be replaced with frozen cranberries too.

Nutritional Information per Serving:

Calories: 207 | **Fat:** 14.9g | **Sat Fat:** 1.3g | **Carbohydrates:** 11.6g | **Fiber:** 2.9g | **Sugar:** 7.4g | **Protein:** 2.5g

Chocolate Muffins

Preparation Time: 15 minutes
Cooking Time: 15 minutes
Servings: 12

Ingredients:

- 1 1/3 cups self-rising flour
- 2/3 cup plus 3 tablespoons caster sugar
- 2½ tablespoons cocoa powder
- 3½ ounces butter
- 5 tablespoons milk
- 2 medium eggs
- ½ teaspoon vanilla extract
- Water, to taste
- ½ ounce milk chocolate, finely chopped

Preparation:

1. In a bowl, mix well flour, sugar, and cocoa powder.
2. With a pastry cutter, cut in the butter until a breadcrumb-like mixture forms.
3. In another bowl, mix together the milk and eggs.
4. Add the egg mixture into flour mixture and mix until well combined.
5. Add the vanilla extract and a little water and mix until well combined.
6. Fold in the chopped chocolate.
7. Grease 12 muffin molds.
8. Transfer mixture evenly into the prepared muffin molds.
9. Arrange the "Crisper Basket" in the pot of Ninja Foodi Grill.
10. Close the Ninja Foodi Grill with lid and select "Air Crisp".
11. Set the temperature to 355 degrees F to preheat.
12. Press "Start/Stop" to begin preheating.
13. When the display shows "Add Food" open the lid and place the muffin molds into the "Crisper Basket".
14. Close the Ninja Foodi Grill with lid and set the time for 9 minutes.
15. Press "Start/Stop" to begin cooking.
16. After 9 minutes of cooking, set the temperature to 320 degrees F for 6 minutes.
17. When the cooking time is completed, press "Start/Stop" to stop cooking and open the lid.
18. Place the muffin molds onto a wire rack to cool for about 10 minutes.
19. Now, invert the muffins onto the wire rack to cool completely before serving.

Serving Suggestions: Garnishing of sprinkles will add a festive touch in these muffins.

Variation Tip: Use room temperature eggs.

Nutritional Information per Serving:

Calories: 389 | **Fat:** 31.2g | **Sat Fat:** 19.5g | **Carbohydrates:** 26.3g | **Fiber:** 0.8g | **Sugar:** 15.1g | **Protein:** 3.2g

Lava Cake

Preparation Time: 15 minutes
Cooking Time: 12½ minutes
Servings: 4

Ingredients:

- 2/3 cup chocolate chips
- ½ cup unsalted butter
- 2 large eggs
- 2 large egg yolks
- 1 cup confectioners' sugar
- 1 teaspoon peppermint extract
- 1/3 cup all-purpose flour plus more for dusting
- 2 tablespoons powdered sugar
- ¼ cup fresh raspberries

Preparation:

1. In a microwave-safe bowl, place the chocolate chips and butter and microwave on High for about 30 seconds.
2. Remove the bowl from microwave and stir the mixture well.
3. Add the eggs, egg yolks and confectioners' sugar and beat until well combined.
4. Add the flour and gently stir to combine.
5. Grease 4 ramekins and dust each with a little flour.
6. Place the chocolate mixture into the prepared ramekins evenly.
7. Arrange the "Crisper Basket" in the pot of Ninja Foodi Grill.
8. Close the Ninja Foodi Grill with lid and select "Air Crisp".
9. Set the temperature to 375 degrees F to preheat.
10. Press "Start/Stop" to begin preheating.
11. When the display shows "Add Food" open the lid and place the ramekins into the "Crisper Basket".
12. Close the Ninja Foodi Grill with lid and set the time for 12 minutes.
13. Press "Start/Stop" to begin cooking.
14. When cooking time is completed, press "Start/Stop" to stop cooking and open the lid.
15. Transfer the ramekins onto a wire rack for about 5 minutes.
16. Carefully run a knife around the sides of each ramekin many times to loosen the cake.
17. Carefully invert each cake onto a dessert plate and dust with powdered sugar.
18. Garnish with raspberries and serve immediately.

Serving Suggestions: Enjoy the lava cake with ice cream.

Variation Tip: For the best result, measure the ingredients with care.

Nutritional Information per Serving:

Calories: 596 | **Fat:** 36.2g | **Sat Fat:** 22g | **Carbohydrates:** 60.1g | **Fiber:** 1.7g | **Sugar:** 19.1g | **Protein:** 8.1g

Chocolate Brownie Cake

Preparation Time: 15 minutes
Cooking Time: 35 minutes
Servings: 6

Ingredients:

- ½ cup dark chocolate chips
- ½ cup butter
- 3 eggs
- ¼ cup sugar
- 1 teaspoon vanilla extract

Preparation:

1. In a microwave-safe bowl, add the chocolate chips and butter and microwave for about 1 minute, stirring after every 20 seconds.
2. Remove from the microwave and stir well.
3. In a bowl, add the eggs, sugar and vanilla extract and blend until light and frothy.
4. Slowly, add the chocolate mixture and beat again until well combined.
5. Place the mixture into a lightly greased springform pan.
6. Arrange the "Crisper Basket" in the pot of Ninja Foodi Grill.
7. Close the Ninja Foodi Grill with lid and select "Air Crisp".
8. Set the temperature to 350 degrees F to preheat.
9. Press "Start/Stop" to begin preheating.
10. When the display shows "Add Food" open the lid and place the springform pan into the "Crisper Basket".
11. Close the Ninja Foodi Grill with lid and set the time for 35 minutes.
12. Press "Start/Stop" to begin cooking.
13. When cooking time is completed, press "Start/Stop" to stop cooking and open the lid.
14. Place the pan onto a wire rack to cool for about 10 minutes.
15. Carefully invert the cake onto the wire rack to cool completely.
16. Cut into desired-sized slices and serve.

Serving Suggestions: Cream cheese frosting will enhance the taste of cake.

Variation Tip: Use the best quality chocolate chips for cake.

Nutritional Information per Serving:

Calories: 247 | **Fat:** 20.2g | **Sat Fat:** 12.1g | **Carbohydrates:** 15.3g | **Fiber:** 0g | **Sugar:** 13.9g | **Protein:** 3.6g

Pumpkin Cake

Preparation Time: 15 minutes
Cooking Time: 40 minutes
Servings: 6

Ingredients:

For Cinnamon Crumb:

- 3 tablespoons all-purpose flour
- 10 teaspoons brown sugar
- 1 teaspoon ground cinnamon
- 1/8 teaspoon salt
- 1½ tablespoons butter, melted

For Cake:

- 1 cup cake flour
- 1 teaspoon baking powder
- ½ teaspoon ground cinnamon
- 6 1/3 tablespoons brown sugar
- 5½ tablespoons unsalted butter, softened
- 1 large egg
- 2/3 cup pumpkin puree

Preparation:

1. For crumb: in a bowl, add all the ingredients except for butter and mix well.
2. Add the melted butter and stir until a crumbly mixture forms.
3. Refrigerate until using.
4. For cake: in a bowl, sift together the flour, baking powder and cinnamon.
5. In another bowl, add the brown sugar and butter and with a hand mixer, beat until creamy.
6. Add the egg and beat until well combined.
7. Add the pumpkin puree and beat until well combined.
8. Add the flour mixture and mix until just combined.
9. Line the bottom of the cake pan with parchment paper.
10. Place the mixture into the prepared cake pan and with a rubber spatula, smooth the top surface.
11. Sprinkle the top of cake with the cinnamon crumb.
12. Arrange the "Crisper Basket" in the pot of Ninja Foodi Grill.
13. Close the Ninja Foodi Grill with lid and select "Air Crisp".
14. Set the temperature to 320 degrees F to preheat.
15. Press "Start/Stop" to begin preheating.

16. When the display shows "Add Food" open the lid and place the pan into the "Crisper Basket".
17. Close the Ninja Foodi Grill with lid and set the time for 40 minutes.
18. Press "Start/Stop" to begin cooking.
19. When cooking time is completed, press "Start/Stop" to stop cooking and open the lid.
20. Place the pan onto a wire rack to cool for about 10 minutes.
21. Carefully invert the cake onto the wire rack to cool completely.
22. Cut into desired-sized slices and serve.

Serving Suggestions: Sprinkle the cake with powdered sugar before serving.

Variation Tip: For the best result, try to use sugar-free pumpkin puree.

Nutritional Information per Serving:

Calories: 298 | **Fat:** 14.6g|**Sat Fat:** 8.9g|**Carbohydrates:** 39.1g|**Fiber:** 1.6g|**Sugar:** 16.1g|**Protein:** 3.8g

Mini Cheesecakes

Preparation Time: 15 minutes
Cooking Time: 10 minutes
Servings: 2

Ingredients:

- ¾ cup Erythritol
- 2 eggs
- 1 teaspoon vanilla extract
- ½ teaspoon fresh lemon juice
- 16 ounces cream cheese, softened
- 2 tablespoon sour cream

Preparation:

1. In a blender, add the Erythritol, eggs, vanilla extract and lemon juice and pulse until smooth.
2. Add the cream cheese and sour cream and pulse until smooth.
3. Place the mixture into 2 (4-inch) springform pans evenly.
4. Arrange the "Crisper Basket" in the pot of Ninja Foodi Grill.
5. Close the Ninja Foodi Grill with lid and select "Air Crisp".
6. Set the temperature to 350 degrees F to preheat.
7. Press "Start/Stop" to begin preheating.
8. When the display shows "Add Food" open the lid and place the pans into the "Crisper Basket".
9. Close the Ninja Foodi Grill with lid and set the time for 10 minutes.
10. Press "Start/Stop" to begin cooking.
11. When cooking time is completed, press "Start/Stop" to stop cooking and open the lid.
12. Place the pans onto a wire rack to cool completely.
13. Refrigerate overnight before serving.

Serving Suggestions: Enjoy with the topping of berry sauce.

Variation Tip: Erythritol can be replaced with brown sugar.

Nutritional Information per Serving:

Calories: 886 | **Fat:** 86g|**Sat Fat:** 52.8g|**Carbohydrates:** 7.2g|**Fiber:** 0g|**Sugar:** 1.1g|**Protein:** 23.1g

Pumpkin Pie

Preparation Time: 10 minutes
Cooking Time: 20 minutes
Servings: 6

Ingredients:

- 1 package pie crust
- 3 eggs
- 1 (15-ounce) can pumpkin
- ¾ cup brown sugar
- 1 teaspoon ground cinnamon
- 1 teaspoon ground ginger
- 1 teaspoon ground nutmeg
- ½ teaspoon ground cloves
- 1 cup light cream

Preparation:

1. Arrange the pie crust into a tart pan and press to smooth.
2. In a large bowl, add the eggs, pumpkin, brown sugar and spices and beat until well combined.
3. Add the light cream and stir to combine.
4. Place the mixture over the crust evenly.
5. Arrange the "Crisper Basket" in the pot of Ninja Foodi Grill.
6. Close the Ninja Foodi Grill with lid and select "Air Crisp".
7. Set the temperature to 320 degrees F to preheat.
8. Press "Start/Stop" to begin preheating.
9. When the display shows "Add Food" open the lid and place the pan into the "Crisper Basket".
10. Close the Ninja Foodi Grill with lid and set the time for 10 minutes.
11. Press "Start/Stop" to begin cooking.
12. Now, set the temperature to 300 degrees F for 10 minutes.
13. When cooking time is completed, press "Start/Stop" to stop cooking and open the lid.
14. Place the pie pan onto a wire rack to cool for about 10-15 minutes before serving.

Serving Suggestions: Serve this pie with the topping of whipped cream.

Variation Tip: Make sure your crust is not too thin and has no cracks.

Nutritional Information per Serving:

Calories: 286 | **Fat:** 13.7g | **Sat Fat:** 5.8g | **Carbohydrates:** 38.1g | **Fiber:** 2.7g | **Sugar:** 27.9g | **Protein:** 4.9g

Pecan Pie

Preparation Time: 15 minutes
Cooking Time: 35 minutes
Servings: 5

Ingredients:

- ¾ cup brown sugar
- ¼ cup caster sugar
- 1/3 cup butter, melted
- 2 large eggs
- 1¾ tablespoons flour
- 1 tablespoon milk
- 1 teaspoon vanilla extract
- 1 cup pecan halves
- 1 frozen pie crust, thawed

Preparation:

1. In a large bowl, mix together the sugars, and butter.
2. Add the eggs and whisk until foamy.
3. Add the flour, milk, and vanilla extract and whisk until well combined.
4. Fold in the pecan halves.
5. Grease a pie pan.
6. Arrange the crust in the bottom of prepared pie pan.
7. Place the pecan mixture over the crust evenly.
8. Arrange the "Crisper Basket" in the pot of Ninja Foodi Grill.
9. Close the Ninja Foodi Grill with lid and select "Air Crisp".
10. Set the temperature to 300 degrees F to preheat.
11. Press "Start/Stop" to begin preheating.
12. When the display shows "Add Food" open the lid and place the pan into the "Crisper Basket".
13. Close the Ninja Foodi Grill with lid and set the time for 22 minutes.
14. Press "Start/Stop" to begin cooking.
15. Now, set the temperature to 385 degrees F for 13 minutes.
16. When cooking time is completed, press "Start/Stop" to stop cooking and open the lid.
17. Place the pie pan onto a wire rack to cool for about 10-15 minutes before serving.

Serving Suggestions: Vanilla ice cream will go great with this pie.

Variation Tip: This pie is delicious warm or at room temperature.

Nutritional Information per Serving:

Calories: 501 | **Fat:** 35g | **Sat Fat:** 10.8g | **Carbohydrates:** 44.7g | **Fiber:** 2.9g | **Sugar:** 36.7g | **Protein:** 6.2g

Apple Bread Pudding

Preparation Time: 15 minutes
Cooking Time: 22 minutes
Servings: 8

Ingredients:

For Bread Pudding:

- 10½ ounces bread, cubed
- ½ cup apple, peeled, cored and chopped
- ½ cup raisins
- ¼ cup walnuts, chopped
- 1½ cups milk
- ¾ cup water
- 5 tablespoons honey
- 2 teaspoons ground cinnamon
- 2 teaspoons cornstarch
- 1 teaspoon vanilla extract

For Topping:

- 1 1/3 cups plain flour
- 3/5 cup brown sugar
- 7 tablespoons butter

Preparation:

1. In a large bowl, mix together the bread, apple, raisins, and walnuts.
2. In another bowl, add the remaining pudding ingredients and mix until well combined.
3. Add the milk mixture into the bread mixture and mix until well combined.
4. Refrigerate for about 15 minutes, tossing occasionally.
5. For topping: in a bowl, mix together the flour and sugar.
6. With a pastry cutter, cut in the butter until a crumbly mixture forms.
7. Place the mixture into 2 baking pans and spread the topping mixture on top of each.
8. Arrange the "Crisper Basket" in the pot of Ninja Foodi Grill.
9. Close the Ninja Foodi Grill with lid and select "Air Crisp".
10. Set the temperature to 355 degrees F to preheat.
11. Press "Start/Stop" to begin preheating.
12. When the display shows "Add Food" open the lid and place the pans into the "Crisper Basket".
13. Close the Ninja Foodi Grill with lid and set the time for 22 minutes.
14. Press "Start/Stop" to begin cooking.

15. When cooking time is completed, press "Start/Stop" to stop cooking and open the lid.
16. Serve warm.

Serving Suggestions: Sprinkle with nuts of your choice before serving.

Variation Tip: Pear can replace apple in this recipe.

Nutritional Information per Serving:

Calories: 432 | **Fat:** 14.8g|**Sat Fat:** 7.4g|**Carbohydrates:** 69.1g|**Fiber:** 2.8g|**Sugar:** 32g|**Protein:** 7.9g

Pumpkin Bread Pudding

Preparation Time: 15 minutes
Cooking Time: 40 minutes
Servings: 6

Ingredients:

For Pudding:

- ¾ cup heavy cream
- 1/3 cup whole milk
- ½ cup canned pumpkin puree
- 1/3 cup sugar
- 1 large egg
- 1 egg yolk
- ½ teaspoon pumpkin pie spice
- 1/8 teaspoon salt
- 4 cups day-old baguette, cubed
- 4 tablespoons unsalted butter, melted

For Sauce:

- ½ cup heavy cream
- 1/3 cup pure maple syrup
- 1 tablespoon unsalted butter
- ½ teaspoon vanilla extract

Preparation:

1. For pudding: in a bowl, add the cream, milk, pumpkin puree, sugar, egg, egg yolk, pumpkin pie spice and salt and beat until well combined.
2. In another large bowl, add the bread cubes and melted butter and toss to coat well.
3. Add the pumpkin mixture and gently toss to coat.
4. Transfer mixture to an ungreased 6-inch round baking pan.
5. Arrange the "Crisper Basket" in the pot of Ninja Foodi Grill.
6. Close the Ninja Foodi Grill with lid and select "Air Crisp".
7. Set the temperature to 350 degrees F to preheat.
8. Press "Start/Stop" to begin preheating.
9. When the display shows "Add Food" open the lid and place the pan into the "Crisper Basket".
10. Close the Ninja Foodi Grill with lid and set the time for 40 minutes.
11. Press "Start/Stop" to begin cooking.
12. Meanwhile, for sauce: in a small saucepan, add the maple syrup and butter over medium heat and cook until butter is melted, stirring continuously.

13. Stir in the heavy cream and simmer for about 15 minutes, stirring occasionally.
14. Remove from the heat and set aside to cool slightly.
15. When cooking time is completed, press "Start/Stop" to stop cooking and open the lid.
16. Serve warm with the topping of sauce.

Serving Suggestions: You can enjoy this bread pudding with the topping of custard.

Variation Tip: Crusty country bread can also be used instead of a baguette.

Nutritional Information per Serving:

Calories: 358 | **Fat:** 21.7g|**Sat Fat:** 12.8g|**Carbohydrates:** 38.1g|**Fiber:** 1.2g|**Sugar:** 24.3g|**Protein:** 4.7g

Meal Plan for 30 Days

Day 1
Breakfast: Pumpkin Bread

Lunch: Rosemary Scallops

Dinner: Turkey & Yogurt Casserole

Day 2
Breakfast: Spinach & Egg Bites

Lunch: Green Beans Casserole

Dinner: Glazed Salmon

Day 3
Breakfast: Sausage & Scallion Frittata

Lunch: Stuffed Tomatoes

Dinner: Glazed Pork Ribs

Day 4
Breakfast: Eggs with Ham

Lunch: Shrimp Scampi

Dinner: Roasted Chicken with Potatoes

Day 5
Breakfast: Bacon & Kale Cups

Lunch: Vegetarian Stuffed Bell Peppers

Dinner: Buttered Halibut

Day 6
Breakfast: Chicken & Broccoli Quiche

Lunch: Nutty Acorn Squash

Dinner: Pork Loin with Potatoes

Day 7
Breakfast: Savory Carrot Muffins

Lunch: Tofu with Orange Sauce

Dinner: Glazed Salmon

Day 8

Breakfast: Pumpkin Bread

Lunch: Shrimp Kabobs

Dinner: Sweet & Sour Lamb Chops

Day 9

Breakfast: Eggs with Ham

Lunch: Vinegar Brussels Sprout

Dinner: Spinach Stuffed Chicken Breasts

Day 10

Breakfast: Spinach & Egg Bites

Lunch: Beef Stuffed Bell Peppers

Dinner: Buttermilk Brined Turkey Breast

Day 11

Breakfast: Sausage & Scallion Frittata

Lunch: Shrimp Scampi

Dinner: Herbed Beef Roast

Day 12

Breakfast: Eggs with Ham

Lunch: Stuffed Potatoes

Dinner: Sweet & Sour Chicken Drumsticks

Day 13

Breakfast: Chicken & Broccoli Quiche

Lunch: Lemony Green Beans

Dinner: Glazed Pork Ribs

Day 14

Breakfast: Mushroom Frittata

Lunch: Scallops in Caper Sauce

Dinner: sausage Stuffed Chicken Breast

Day 15

Breakfast: Pumpkin Bread

Lunch: Stuffed Potatoes

Dinner: Pesto Rack of Lamb

Day 16

Breakfast: Savory Carrot Muffins

Lunch: Parmesan Shrimp

Dinner: Glazed Ham

Day 17

Breakfast: Pumpkin Bread

Lunch: Scallops in Capers Sauce

Dinner: Buttered Turkey Breast

Day 18

Breakfast: Bacon & Kale Cups

Lunch: Lemony Green Beans

Dinner: Teriyaki Salmon

Day 19

Breakfast: Savory Carrot Muffins

Lunch: Shrimp Kabobs

Dinner: Pork & Sausage Meatloaf

Day 20

Breakfast: Sausage & Scallion Frittata

Lunch: Vinegar Brussels Sprout

Dinner: Glazed Haddock

Day 21

Breakfast: Savory Carrot Muffins

Lunch: Beef Stuffed Bell Peppers

Dinner: Thyme Turkey Tenderloins

Day 22

Breakfast: Mushroom Frittata

Lunch: Glazed Calamari

Dinner: Seasoned Rib-Eye Steak

Day 23

Breakfast: Chicken & Broccoli Quiche

Lunch: Vegetarian Stuffed Bell Peppers

Dinner: Spice Tilapia

Day 24

Breakfast: Spinach & Egg Bites

Lunch: Shrimp Kabobs

Dinner: BBQ Chicken Breasts

Day 25

Breakfast: Sausage & Kale Frittata

Lunch: Green Beans Casserole

Dinner: Glazed leg of Lamb

Day 26

Breakfast: Pumpkin Bread

Lunch: Glazed Calamari

Dinner: Roasted Cornish Hen

Day 27

Breakfast: Eggs with Ham

Lunch: Rosemary Scallops

Dinner: turkey Roll

Day 28

Breakfast: Mushroom Frittata

Lunch: Tofu with Orange Sauce

Dinner: Bacon-Wrapped Beef Tenderloin

Day 29

Breakfast: Bacon & Kale Cups

Lunch: Herbed Mushrooms

Dinner: Zesty Salmon

Day 30

Breakfast: Spinach & Egg Bites

Lunch: Parmesan Shrimp

Dinner: Beef Casserole

Conclusion

Did you like all those meaty feasts, juicy and tender poultry, and seafood delights? Do you love you to enjoy veggies with exceptional flavors? Then bring this inside grill home. This appliance can meet all your Air fryer, Oven, and Grill needs. The Ninja Foodi Grill is the ultimate solution to all your cooking modes and recipes. It is very much safer and convenient to use in comparison to its competitors. It can efficiently perform functions like roasting, baking, grilling, air crisping, and dehydration, etc., with a single touch of a button. It is the ultimate answer to your kitchen needs and provides you with the perfect taste, aroma, and healthiest meals in a very lesser time.Once you get your hands on this indoor grill, try the best of the recipes from the cookbook and spread the joy of good flavors.

Made in the USA
Middletown, DE
30 December 2020